LONDON DISPLAYED

A complete *Stationers' Almanack* sheet with calendar text and steel engraved headpiece. (For headpiece description see **1850** in Catalogue). Significant dates are printed in red; from this practice comes the term 'red letter days'. 645 x 515 mm.

LONDON DISPLAYED

Headpieces from the *Stationers' Almanacks*

by

Ralph Hyde

Publication No. 170
London Topographical Society
2010

LONDON TOPOGRAPHICAL SOCIETY
3 Meadway Gate
London NW11 7LA
2010

ISBN
0 902087 57 6

PRODUCED IN GREAT BRITAIN BY
OUTSET SERVICES LIMITED

CONTENTS

FOREWORD

RALPH HYDE was Keeper of Prints and Maps at Guildhall Library for over twenty-five years. No one knew or knows more about illustrations of London than he. He has long interested himself in sheet almanacks with engraved headpieces of London buildings and views published by the Stationers' Company. No one had seemed even to notice, let alone wonder why there were sometimes two different views in a single year. That the Company should publish two, one with a headpiece, the other a workaday calendar and almanack, might have made commercial sense, but the variant headpieces made no sense at all, until Ralph solved the mystery by setting out to track down and catalogue every surviving specimen. In doing so he discovered that there were different series, seemingly only one of them published by the Company.

These engraved almanacks are now, like all ephemera, rare and, like all annual publications, they were generally discarded when the next year's appeared, so it is unsurprising that hardly any library has a long run, let alone a complete set; in addition, they easily fall prey to cannibals who cut off their decorative headpieces, discarding the almanack itself and with it most of the useful evidence of publication. There is a sad instance of this within the library of the Stationers' Company.

It was not until the mid-1970s that the Stationers' Company set up a library (its archive goes back to 1556) in an attic room above the Court Room, with books donated by members of the livery; but there was no shelving, nor any money to buy any. How could it be raised? The library Trustees looked round for something to sell and their eyes lighted on two long runs of Stationers' Company sheet almanacks, apparently duplicates. The bookseller and print dealer, Ben Weinreb, made them an offer. Bookseller and vendors were delighted, the latter, however, not for long. Too late was it realized that the sets were not, or at least not entirely, duplicates, but by then Ben had smartly whipped off their heads and sold them to eager customers at a good price. The Trustees could not even offer to buy them back and had, in any case, already spent the money on the shelving. Alas for the Company, alas for Ralph Hyde when he started ferreting around in Stationers' Hall, Guildhall, the British Library, the British Museum and elsewhere, trying to reconstruct the original long runs. How much easier would his search have been had the two sets sat side by side in the Company's library where he could quietly have compared them in lunch hours snatched from his work round the corner at Guildhall. He might then have reached his revelatory conclusion years ago.

Nor did the records of the Stationers' Company give as much help as might have been expected, considering how complete an archive they are in most areas of the Company's activity. On the detailed operation of the English Stock, they are curiously silent. It seems odd that the records of this key operation of the Company are so sparse and patchy; the board apparently kept next to no account of their monthly committee meetings until 1869, apart from one solitary minute book, 1755–66; nor did they keep regular sales accounts until 1801. This made disentangling the story far from easy, and Ralph had to build up most of the evidence from surviving copies of the almanacks themselves.

But build it up he did, establishing that there were three distinct runs, four if we include the exquisite miniature *London* or *Raven Almanack*. (The Stationers' archive contains a volume of proof pulls complete from 1704, when the English Stock took it over from the bookseller, Joseph Raven.) Only one of the large sheet *Stationers' Almanacks* is official, bearing the Company's own imprint. Another is published by John Scatcherd (later Scatcherd and Whitaker) bookseller, and tenant of the Company at 12 Ave Maria Lane. The third series was put out by Edward Ryland, copper-plate engraver. The puzzle is that the non-Stationers' Company series do not seem to be outright pirates. The Stationers took no reprisals or legal action to stop them, as they would quickly have done in such cases. So we are both nearer and no nearer — we know there were the variant series, but we do not know what their relationship was to each other.

The story, as told in Ralph's introduction, makes good and informative reading as the lead-in to the reproductions of these decorative engravings, which please the eye and show us corners of London which may be known or unknown to us, or which have long vanished in successive tides of war and building development.

Robin Myers
(Archivist Emeritus to the
Worshipful Company of Stationers
& Newspaper Makers)
London, March 2010

Detail from a leporello, *A Railway Adventure [of] Mr Larkins*, published by Ackermann & Co., *c*.1850. This scene shows Lionel Larkins, City clerk, in his office. The *Stationers' Almanack* graces the wall.

ACKNOWLEDGEMENTS

2009 saw the reorganization of Guildhall Library with its prints, drawings, maps, photographs and ephemera being transferred to the London Metropolitan Archives (LMA). The LMA, already in possession of a rich collection of such material (inherited in the main from the London County Council) is thus the home today of what must surely be the most extensive collection of images relating to a single city. Seventy-eight of the images described in this catalogue are from that source.

The author would like to express special thanks to the Chairman of the London Topographical Society, Dr Penelope Hunting, who served as the editor of this volume; Denise Silvester-Carr for sub-editing it; Laurence Worms for providing information on engravers from his files; Jeremy Smith of the London Metropolitan Archives for organizing the photography of the bulk of the illustrations; and Graham Maney for the book's production. Invaluable help was also given by the late Bernard Adams, Bob Aspinall, Michael Ball, Ruth Barriskill, David Beasley, Paul Bentley, Wendy Bennett, the Hon. Christopher Lennox-Boyd, Richard Bowden, Diana Brook, David Milbank Challis, Carol Deton, Joan Dormer, Julian I. Edison, Ian Fletcher, Keith Fletcher, Mireille Galinou, Jonathan Gestetner, Rosemary Hill, Jolyon Hudson, Keith Jackson, the late Peter Jackson, Valerie Jackson-Harris, Richard Knight, Joselyn McDiarmid, Robin Myers MBE, Christoper Nicholson, Sheila O'Connell, the late J. F. C. Phillips, Professor Michael Port, Nicholas Potter, Lady (Jane) Roberts, John A. Robins, Dr Ann Saunders, Nicola Smith, Richard Shaw, Kay Staniland, Nigel Talbot, Bob Thomson, Pieter van der Merwe, David Webb and Alex Werner.

INTRODUCTION

An emblematical headpiece for the *Stationers' Almanack* commemorating the birth of a royal infant, the future George IV. Line engraving. Published by E. Ryland, 1762.

THE STATIONERS' ALMANACK was not designed to be put in your pocket. It was designed to be displayed on the wall where people would see it and consult it for its useful information and enjoy looking at the engraved view. Throughout the nineteenth century the views were predominately of London. Hence my choice of title — *London Displayed*. These engravings were too attractive to throw away and at the end of the year when the almanack was taken down and replaced the engraving on the old almanack would be cut out and the rest disposed of. You will find plenty of examples in the portfolios of London prints at London print dealers. Lacking their headings and sometimes their titles, you can be forgiven for not knowing what they are. They are very cheap but they are potentially very useful to London historians and attractive to collectors. This book will provide you with the means for identifying each of the London engravings of the *Stationers' Almanacks*.

Pre-history

Let me briefly set the scene. Wynkyn de Worde is credited with printing the first almanack in England in 1498. In 1557 the Worshipful Company of Stationers was incorporated. James I would grant the Company Letters Patent for the sole printing of primers, psalters and also almanacks. The monopoly, which appeared to be perpetual, was designed to provide 'help and relief of the Masters, Wardens, Freemen or Commonalty and their successors for ever'. In other words, it would provide the Company with a welcome source of income. That made almanacks important. Charles I in 1635 made the universities of Oxford and Cambridge the Stationers' co-monopolists. In 1711 an Almanack Stamp Duty was imposed. Since the Stationers' Company alone had the capital to lay in stocks of stamped paper, Stamp Duty worked to its advantage.

I

In any case, almanacks rapidly became big business. They were cheap to produce, and every year anyone who had bought one last year would need to buy a replacement. Their publication was the responsibility of the English Stock, a wholesale company which operated within the Stationers' Company from 1603 to 1961. Numbers printed in the eighteenth century remained constant at between 350,000 and 400,000. In 1830, according to the Stationers' Company's statistics, 452,450 were printed. By then the Stationers had about twenty-five different almanack titles. *Old Moore*, the most popular of them all, sold as many as 270,000 copies annually.

Precursors

Most almanacks were printed on inferior paper: some were almost illegible. Book almanacks were designed to be carried in the pocket. On the Continent another category was available — sheet almanacks, designed to be pinned to the wall. These supplied calendar information in a small area usually at bottom centre. The remaining area was occupied by an elaborate engraving. In France large sheet almanacks were published year by year throughout Louis XIV's reign. The engravings on them celebrated in a riot of Baroque allegory the monarch's wars and glorious victories, and just occasionally the benefits of peace. Louis is depicted on them directing battles he had never been to. These almanacks were pure propaganda.[1]

The first serious sheet almanack in Britain was the *Oxford Almanack*, launched in 1674. It is still being published today. The 1674 almanack was large — it was printed from four copper plates — and carried an impressive amount of useful and slightly less useful information: the 'Chief Ports in and about England'; a 'Table of Marriage'; a 'Table of Interest at the Rate of Six in a Hundred'; and so on. The image on it consisted of a hollow circular tower rising from the sea. Within it was a tall obelisk inscribed with the names of all the English monarchs (the 'regal list'). Classical deities, symbolizing the months, reclined on clouds, together with personifications of the four seasons. The design has fairly confidently been attributed to Robert Streeter, the decorative artist responsible for painting the splendid ceiling in the Sheldonian Theatre.

Subsequent *Oxford Almanacks* were printed from a single plate and, compared with the continental models, were restrained. They were allegorical, each a scholarly exercise designed to enhance the prestige of the University. Michael Burghers, Oxford's *calcographus academicus*, designed and engraved most of the early ones, being succeeded by George Vertue, engraver to the Society of Antiquaries. On at least one occasion the artist was James Thornhill. The engravers included Claude Du Bosc and Gerard Vandergucht. Allegory gave way in the 1720s to architectural topics, and later on to topography. In the 1750s and 1760s Samuel Wale was the regular designer, and in the 1770s and 1780s the highly competent Rookers, Edward the father, and Michael Angelo the son. The young J. M. W. Turner made ten drawings for the almanack, nine of which were engraved. The Delegates were less impressed by them than they should have been.[2]

In London, the Stationers' Company dragged its heels. The demand was for almanack books, supplying horoscopes, doggerel rhymes, medical advice, prophecies and such like. Though hugely popular, they were not considered entirely respectable. Amongst this mass of almanacks there was one exception — a thoroughly respectable sheet almanack called the *London Almanack*, sometimes *Raven's Almanack*. This supplied calendar information — weeks and months, with red letter days and moon changes, a table of kings and queens, a list of lord mayors and sheriffs of the City of London, and interest tables — but its most attractive feature was its engraved, allegorical headpiece. The almanack measured only 262 × 214 mm. What was one supposed to do with it? Leave it lying flat on one's desk? More probably it was folded carefully along the columns and tucked into one's pocket.[3] Covers were called for or it would soon become tatty so it became common practice for purchasers to have them dissected and bound. Today they are collected not just for their engravings, but as miniature books and for their exquisite decorative bindings[4] (see p. 75).

Arrival of the Stationers' Almanack

It was not until 1746 that a large sheet almanack to be compared to the *Oxford Almanack* at last made its appearance in London. This was the *Stationers' Almanack*.

Surviving eighteenth-century examples of the *Stationers' Almanack* are excessively scarce. Some I have been unable to find. That is true of the very first one. The following advertisement appeared in the *London Evening Post*, 20–2 November 1746:

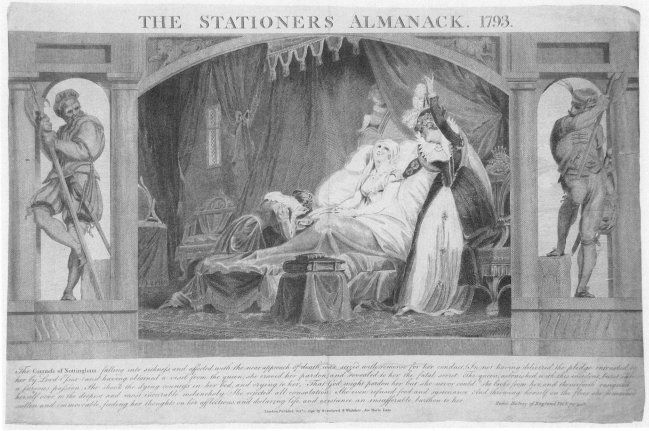

The Countess of Nottingham *falling into sickness and affected with the near approach of death, was seized with remorse for her conduct, In not having delivered the pledge entrusted to her by Lord Essex; and having obtained a visit from the queen; she craved her pardon, and revealed to her the fatal secret. The queen, astonished with this incident, burst into a furious passion; She shook the dying countess in her bed, and crying to her, 'That God might pardon her; but she never could' she broke from her, and thenceforth remained herself over to the deepest and most incurable melancholy. She rejected all consolation; She even refused food and sustenance. And throwing herself on the floor she remained sullen and immoveable, feeding her thoughts on her afflictions, and declaring life and existence an insufferable burthen to her.* Hume's History of England Vol.I. p. 456

London, Publish'd Oct.r 1. 1792 by Scatcherd & Whitaker, Ave Maria Lane

An historical headpiece for a *Stationers' Almanack*. Line engraving. Published 1 October 1792 by Scatcherd & Whitaker.

This Day is published,
With the Consent of the Company of
Stationers,
and the Commissioners of the Stamp-Office.
Price 1s. On fine Paper 1s.6d.
THE STATIONERS' ALMANACK, for the
Year 1747

The Proprietor has made it not only useful but has embellished it with a curious Print of his Royal Highness the DUKE, attended by Victory and Minerva presenting him to Britannia; at his feet lies Rebellion in the Figure of a Highlander; on one side are Tyranny and Superstition, flying from Britannia; and on the other side is the Ambition of France with her Wings clipped; behind her are the Walls of Culloden-House and in the Heavens the Sign of Taurus denotes at once the happy Time of the Duke's Birth, and of his crushing the late unnatural Rebellion. The whole is a genteel Decoration for a Parlour, Compting-house or Closet.

And it is printed by Edward Ryland, in Half-Moon Court, next Ludgate; and sold by S. Birt, B. Dob, R. Baldwin and Co. and W. Baker and Son, near Stationers'-Hall.

A handbill in the British Library announces the *Stationers' Almanack* for 1749. It would be

published on 22 November (in other words, 'Almanack Day' — see below), and be number IV. Assuming that the almanack was being published regularly, the first must have been published in 1745 for 1746.

As we see from the above, the almanack for 1747 was allegorical. It celebrated the victory of the Duke of Cumberland, second son of George II, over the forces of the Young Pretender, Bonnie Prince Charlie, at the Battle of Culloden on 16 April 1746. In other words it is patriotic and triumphalist. For the next twelve months it would proclaim its Hanoverian, anti-Jacobite message in 'Parlours, Compting houses and Closets' throughout the land.

Note that the *Stationers' Almanack* at this stage is not being published by the Stationers' Company itself, but with its *consent*.[5] Frequently it is dedicated to the current Lord Mayor. The dedicator is Ryland, not the Company. That suggests that Ryland was not only the printer but also the publisher. By 1768 Ryland is actually describing himself as the almanack's publisher — he sometimes names himself as engraver, too. Yet this is at a time when the Company jealously guarded and vigorously defended its unique rights to almanack publication. At top centre of the engraved frame[6] you will see the arms of the Stationers' Company. Are the arms some sort of assertion? How do we interpret it? What was the arrangement between the two parties? It is all very odd.

The Museum of London has a copy of the almanack for 1752. In this year the headpiece is no longer allegorical but historical. It depicts the legendary incident that gave rise to the Order of the Garter. Edward III, at a ball in Calais in 1348, has just lifted the garter dropped by the future Princess of Wales. Tying it below his knee, he uttered the words, 'Honi soi qui mal y pense'. In the calendar area of the almanack the signs of the zodiac appear above the months. The regal column on the left is headed by a royal crown, and the episcopal column on the right is headed by a bishop's mitre. The copper plate would be reused for the almanack for 1783.

For the 1769 almanack Ryland helped himself to an existing allegorical composition — the one that decorates the pedestal of the Monument. The rebuilding of the City after the Great Fire of 1666 provided a perfect almanack theme — a mixture of civic pride and heady patriotism: joy at the speedy recovery of the City, pride at its new architecture.

The prolific illustrator and decorative painter, Samuel Wale, who was producing designs for the *Oxford Almanack*, also provided Mary Ryland, Edward's widow and successor, with designs, both allegorical and historical, for the *Stationers' Almanack*. With the *Oxford Almanacks* scholarly customers with classical educations were often left to work out the meanings of the classical compositions. In the City of London such knowledge could not be assumed, and long explanations appear in the bottom margins. Britannia, attended by Neptune and the tritons, features frequently, as does London personified (a female figure wearing a mural crown), and the Thames (a reclining river god, with an urn from which water issues). Commerce for the City is all-important, and cornucopias regularly spill forth their riches. As the century progresses and overseas territories are acquired, the benefits of British imperialism are emphasized, and defending such territories from other European powers justified.

Towards the close of the eighteenth century a new species of *Stationers' Almanack* headpiece appears. Examples in this species are engravings of naval and military battles. Some are important, but many of them are of military incidents that undoubtedly were important at the time but have been consigned to history's dustbin. For a while there was a vogue for history paintings of expiring British officers. For example, on 6 January 1781 a contingent of French soldiers invaded Jersey. It was the final attempt by French forces to seize the island. In a tussle in Royal Square, St Helier, a British officer, Major Francis Pierson, was killed. Alderman John Boydell, printmaker and Master of the Stationers' Company in 1783–4, encouraged John Singleton Copley to record this incident. The first proof after Copley's resulting painting was issued by Boydell on 1 September 1788. Interestingly, the *Stationers' Almanack* recorded the same incident on its headpiece for 1789, but their image was drawn by Edward Francis Burney and was totally different[7] (see plate opposite). Copley's version was not actually published until 1796.

Thomas Carnan sees off 'perpetual copyright'

We have seen how the Stationers' Company vigorously guarded its privilege to publish almanacks. The publication of counterfeit and 'sham' almanacks was a recurring problem. In the 1770s this problem came to a head when perpetual copyright was challenged by a rogue bookseller named Thomas Carnan, who took out an injunction against the Company, arguing that James I had no power to grant a perpetual monopoly. In 1775 the judges gave their opinion that the Company's right could not be exclusive. Carnan triumphed and a great mass of new almanacks and outright piracies was published, many but not all of them by Carnan. Among the non-Carnan almanacks was a second *Stationers' Almanack*, which carried the name Scatcherd. 'The Death of Major Pierson' had been one such. James Scatcherd was a bookseller and Common Councilman operating from Ave Maria Lane. In some imprints his firm appears as Scatcherd & Whitaker or Scatcherd & Letterman. Thus from this point until the 1820s there were two rival *Stationers' Almanacks* being published.[8]

In the meantime, Ryland's almanacks continued to carry the arms of the Company, hinting at a semi-official status. Scatcherd's do not display the Company's arms. Nevertheless their 1789 almanack carries the words, 'Printed by Permission of the Company of Stationers'. Quite clearly, they enjoyed the approval of Alderman John Boydell. In 1790 Boydell was elected Lord Mayor. On the almanack for 1791 Scatcherd & Whitaker humbly dedicate their almanack to 'the Right Honourable John Boydell, Lord Mayor of the City of London, and to the Worshipful Company of Stationers'.

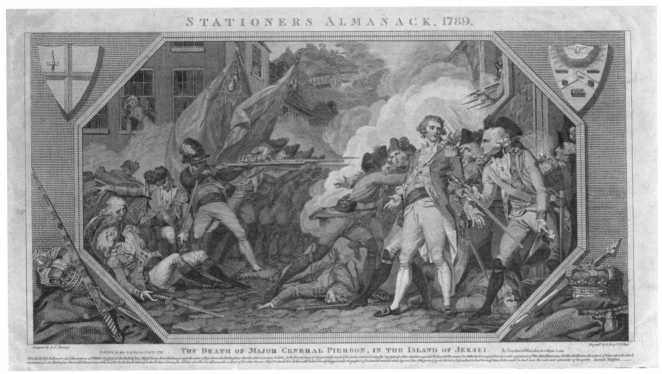

A military headpiece for a *Stationers' Almanack*. Line engraving. Published 14 December 1788 by Scatcherd & Whitaker.

The Napoleonic Wars

Allegorical designs were now out of fashion. After producing several almanacks with jingoistic historical subjects, both Scatcherd and the Ryland family applied themselves almost exclusively to headpieces with jingoistic military topics. Concern about Napoleon's ambitions led to the raising in London of volunteer units. Scatcherd published a headpiece showing the review of the volunteer corps in Hyde Park in 1799, and another dealing with the review that took place on Blackheath in 1805. Nelson's Attack on Copenhagen, the Battle before Alexandria, the Battle of Barbarosa, the Battle of Badajoz, the Battle of Vittoria and the Battle of San Sebastian were all illustrated. So, too, was the London visit of the Tsar Alexander I, and the King of Prussia in the summer of 1814 when the victory over Napoleon was prematurely celebrated. The story was brought to a close with a headpiece entitled 'England Triumphant. Bonaparte Vainly Endeavouring to Rally his Imperial Guards', and engraved by J. Edwards after J. A. Atkinson for the 1816 almanack.

Metropolitan Improvements I

Once Napoleon was safely confined to St Helena, publishers turned their attention from matters military to matters pacific. There was 'The Coronation of George the Fourth' to be celebrated, and then 'His Majesty's Embarkation at Greenwich, for Scotland, August 10th 1822' — the so-called 'Northern Excursion'. The completion of several new structures was celebrated, too — Waterloo Bridge which opened in 1817, David Laing's new Custom House which also opened in 1817 and Southwark Bridge which opened in 1819. The new bridges would lead to the rapid development of South London.

'Metropolitan Improvement' were the buzz words of the 1820s. Marylebone Park had reverted to the Crown in 1811 at the expiry of a long lease. In the hands of the Prince Regent's favourite architect, John Nash, Regent's Park would become an aristocratic garden city with long stucco terraces surrounding it. The Colosseum with its London panorama would be built there as well. To lure people to the park, Regent Street and Portland Place would be built. At the southern end of this street was the Regent's palace, Carlton House. This would be demolished. Buckingham House would be rebuilt as Buckingham Palace as his residence. Wellington Arch would be built by Decimus Burton at Hyde Park Corner as an entrance to the avenue leading to the Palace. Other new developments would include new government offices, the University of London (i.e., University

College), a new General Post Office, and New London Bridge. All these improvements would be celebrated on headpieces for the *Stationers' Almanacks*. In the 1830s there would be a new Goldsmiths' Hall, the National Gallery and Trafalgar Square, and what was proclaimed to be (though it sounds odd now) the City's answer to Regent Street, King William Street, linking New London Bridge to Bank.

There was a great thirst for knowledge and self-improvement. A Society for the Diffusion of Useful Knowledge (SDUK), closely associated with the recently founded University College, was launched in 1826. It devoted itself to providing inexpensive texts for the rapidly expanding reading public, and its publications included *The Penny Magazine*, an SDUK atlas and the *British Almanac*. The *British Almanac* was in a different class entirely to the wretched prognostications issued in vast numbers by the Stationers' Company as book almanacks. The *Athenaeum* carried a review of the SDUK's almanack, using it as the vehicle for a savage onslaught on the Stationers' Company. It was reprinted in *The Times* on 3 January 1828. The reviewer described their almanacks as 'a farrago of filth, obscenity and stupidity'. Strange it was indeed that so respected a body could lay itself open to the charge of circulating obscenity. The Stationers were already reacting to such criticism. On 13 December 1825 they had announced in *The Times* that they had taken over Scatcherd's firm and that from now on the *Stationers' Almanack* would be theirs, printed and sold for them by G. Greenhill at Stationers' Hall.[9]

> They [the Worshipful Company of Stationers] rely on the character which their Publications have ever borne for accuracy and utility, for their maintaining their old pre-eminence over all competitors. It is their intention to make the fullest allowance to all dealers; and to take back any Almanacks which are unsold and unsoiled, if returned before the 16th day of February 1835 ...[10]

(The Company in 1869 would take over the *British Almanac*, too).

The improvement of the two *Stationers' Almanacks* was also assisted by what happened to stamp duties. By 1834 for sheet almanacks the duty was at its highest but an increasing number of almanacks were evading the duty. In its battle against rivals, the Stationers' Company chose to press Parliament for further stamp duty. To its dismay, however, Parliament responded by declaring the Company's privilege outmoded and abolished the tax altogether.

As a result, the price of both *Stationers' Almanacks* was reduced from 3*s*. 6*d*. to 2*s*. (Proof impressions of the official headpieces, printed on thick paper, sold for 3*s*.).[11]

One consequence of the Company's change of direction was a marked improvement of the engraved headpieces. A new artist, Thomas Higham, was engaged to draw and engrave theirs. His first was a 'View in the Regent's Park' showing York Terrace, Cornwall Terrace, Sussex Place and Hanover Terrace. Higham, born in Bramfield in Suffolk, had been apprenticed to the London engraver and antiquary John Grieg. He is considered to have been one of the most accomplished engravers of the day.[12] His fellow engraver, James Charles Armytage, referred to Higham's view of Rouen Cathedral as 'one of the plates of the century'.[13] Higham would draw and/or engrave every one of the official *Stationers' Almanacks* from this date until his early death in 1844. The final ones were mainly after drawings by George Moore who lithographed Charles Robert Cockerell's astonishing competition designs for the Royal Exchange — 'a triumphal Arch made habitable by floors'.

The Stationers may have taken over Scatcherd's, but they had not taken over the original *Stationers' Almanack*, published since 1746 by members of the Ryland family. The almanack for 1819 shows the Ryland family still hanging on. It was published by J. Robins & Co., Ivy Lane, Paternoster Row; C. Ryland, 83 Cannon Street and J. Robins & Sons, 59 Tooley Street. The almanack for 1824, however, is published by J. Robins alone. With the Stationers' Company vigorously promoting their much-improved almanack, J. Robins & Sons were obliged to radically improve theirs, too. Rather than engage one good artist, they commissioned several. The first was Augustus Pugin, the French émigré architectural artist who had provided the topographical detail in the hundred plates in Rudolph Ackermann's *Microcosm of London* (1808–10). He had also designed the Diorama, Regent's Park and the Cosmorama in Regent Street. Pugin provided drawings for a headpiece featuring the Palace of Westminster and Westminster Abbey; the 'New Palace, St. James's Park' (i.e., Nash's new Buckingham Palace), and New London Bridge. Hyde Park Corner was engraved after a drawing by 'Schrubellie', surely Robert Blemmel Schnebbelie, a very fine topographical artist who had worked for Robert

Candidate design for a *Stationers' Almanack* headpiece by Thomas Allom, showing the Tower of London and the Custom House. Pen and wash drawing, *c*.1840.

Wilkinson on *Londina Illustrata* (1819–34). The Havell family were also engaged by Robins. 'Covent Garden Market' and 'Greenwich Hospital' were drawn by William and Frederick James Havell, and engraved by Frederick James Havell. Robert Havell Junior took a day off from printing Audubon's *Birds of America* to go to Greenwich on 4 May 1832 and record King William and Queen Adelaide's 'Royal Aquatic Excursion'. Frederick James Havell's plate seems to show the aftermath of the occasion, with some vessels still there and the crowd dispersing. William Havell also visited Greenwich and drew the Greenwich Naval Hospital from the top of Greenwich Hill. The line of young ladies suggests it was Whit Monday when day-trippers headed for Greenwich and the fittest of them linked arms and hurtled themselves down the hill.

Robins' principal artist, however, was the illustrator, panoramist, architect and perspectivist, Thomas Allom.[14] Between 1834 and 1853 Allom provided drawings for almanacks on at least fifteen occasions. Eleven of them were London scenes, described in this catalogue. A pen-and-wash drawing of the Tower of London in the London Metropolitan Archives, formerly in the Guildhall Library collection, can confidently be attributed to Allom. From its dimensions it was obviously intended for the almanack, but for some reason not selected (see plate above). Three non-London scenes by Allom were engraved for the almanack, of Dover, Gravesend and Osborne House.

A regular engraver employed by J. and W. Robins, who engraved after Thomas Allom, the marine artist Edward Duncan and George Chambers Junior, was Thomas Abiel Prior. A meticulous worker, it is said he often took several years to complete a plate. This one can well believe when one studies Chambers' 'City of London, Mansion House, Poultry and Princes Street' (see pp. 56–7).

Almanack Day

A word must be said about Almanack Day, 22 November, the day on which traditionally the Stationers' Company published their almanacks, including the *Stationers' Almanack*, of course. Charles Knight describes the extremely animated scene at Stationers' Hall.

> All over the long table that extends through the hall and piled up in tall heaps on the floor, are canvas bales or bags innumerable ... The doors are locked as yet, but will be opened presently for a novel scene. The clock strikes, wide asunder start the gates, and in they come, a whole army of porters, darting hither and thither, and seizing the said bags, in many instances as big as themselves. Before we can understand what is the matter the hall is clear;

another hour or two and the contents of the latter will be flying along railways, east, west, north and south; yet another day and they will be dispersed throughout every city and town and parish and hamlet of England ...[15]

Use of architects' drawings

Almanacks were concerned with time — the past, the present and the future — so almanack publishers needed to be bang up to date. If they were showing London buildings they had to be new ones, especially new public buildings that were about to be erected. Access had to be made, therefore, to architects' perspectives, the very precise watercolour drawings that architects prepared in order to show their clients how the buildings would look when erected.

George Smith's perspective was copied for the 1823 almanack showing the new pepper-pot tower for the Royal Exchange. Wilkins seems to have lent, or at least allowed access to, his perspectives for the University College headpiece, and for the National Gallery. The Royal Exchange was burnt down on 10 January 1838. When researching the Shepherd family for *Shepherd's London* (London: Cassell, 1976), John Phillips unearthed a letter from Thomas Hosmer Shepherd to William Tite, the architect selected to design the replacement building. It is dated 13 May 1840 and reads:

> Dear Sir,
> Having with pleasure heard from public report that your designs are chosen for building a new Royal Exchange, I have taken the liberty to ask you if you would allow me to have a sketch of the Principal Front, as I think I can get an order for a Drawing for it for the 'Stationers' Almanac' — should I be fortunate enough to obtain your permission I shall feel certainly obliged — I remain Dr. Sir, yours much obliged T.H. Shepherd.
> P.S. I will take the liberty to call or send for an answer in a day or two.[16]

Both almanacks published headpieces of the new Royal Exchange, but neither is signed T. H. Shepherd. Either Tite declined to cooperate with Shepherd or the almanack publishers had other artists in mind.

Charles Barry used Thomas Allom as his perspectivist, and Allom, of course, was regularly supplying J. & W. Robins with drawings for their *Stationers' Almanacks*. It is no surprise, therefore, that a Barry perspective is used for 'The New

Treasury Offices, Whitehall' in 1848. Allom also prepared magnificent perspectives for the new Houses of Parliament, which were presented to Tsar Nicholas I during his State Visit to London in 1842 and are now in the Scientific Research Museum of the Russian Academy of Fine Arts, St Petersburg. When we compare these perspectives with 'Westminster, from Bishop's Walk, Lambeth', we see an unmistakable relationship, particularly where Barry's rejected idea for an extremely tall ventilation tower is concerned.

From the death of Thomas Higham in 1844, the regular engraver for the Company's *Stationers' Almanack* was Henry Adlard. Adlard was born in 1799 in the parish of St Bartholomew-the-Great in London, the son of the printer, James Adlard, who published the engraved key-sheets and descriptive booklets for visitors to Barker and Burford's circular panoramas. Thomas was known principally as a landscape and portrait engraver. He was often called as an expert witness in forgery and deception cases. The census for 1841 records him as being married with six children. From 1845 to 1876 he would engrave all the Company's *Stationers' Almanacks*. Several of the finest are after J. Marchant whose images are crowded with lively human detail, most notably 'The South End of St. James's Street ... on a Drawing Room Day', 'The West Front of the Horse Guards', and 'The Zoological Gardens in the Regent's Park'. He also seems to have had access to architects' perspectives. 'The South Front of the British Museum' credits 'Sir R. Smirke, R.A., Archt.', and is after a drawing by Frederick Mackenzie, who drew the perspectives for James Bunstone Bunning's entry for the Royal Exchange competition, and provided the drawings for twenty-two of the *Oxford Almanacks*. Adlard was seventy-six when he engraved his last almanack for the Stationers' Company. He died in Hackney in 1893 at the age of ninety-four.

From the mid-1840s in the case of Robins' unofficial almanack, and the mid-1850s in the case of the Company's official almanack, non-London subjects began to feature. The official almanack carried river scenes and harbours — Chatham, Milford Haven and Galway Bay — then new buildings such as St George's Hall, Liverpool; and then great engineering triumphs such as the 'Dee Viaduct, Vale of Llangollen', 'Clifton Suspension Bridge' and 'Railway Bridge over the River Tamar'. In the 1860s provincial

'ALMANAC DAY' AT STATIONERS' HALL.

'Almanac Day at Stationers' Hall' from *The Book of Days*, edited by R. Chambers (1878).

towns featured, and from the late 1870s it was cathedrals, all after drawings by the theatre scene painter, John O'Connor.

Metropolitan Improvements II

London continued to provide subjects, nevertheless, particularly in periods of rapid change and development. The 1860s was such a period. In 1866 central London on Cassell's 'Immense Map of London' looks like one extensive building site. Contributing to the upheaval was the construction of underground lines by the Metropolitan and District Railways, the construction by the Metropolitan Board of Works of a system of sewers, and also the construction by the MBW of the Victoria and Albert Embankments and the intrusion into the heart of London for the first time of railway lines,

terminated by huge, prestigious railway hotels. The artist who showed the public the improvements they could expect was John O'Connor, who contributed to the Company's almanack drawings of the Charing Cross Hotel, Cannon Street Station, two of new Government Offices, the Law Courts, and three of the Victoria Embankment. O'Connor's best-loved picture is his atmospheric 'From Pentonville Road looking West: Evening', a foggy scene dominated by St Pancras Station, which is in the Museum of London's collection, but was not engraved for the *Almanack*. The Museum also has an oil version of O'Connor's 'Thames Embankment from Somerset House'. In all probability there was a watercolour or pen and wash version of the image which the engraver copied, and the oil version was painted slightly later. The man

A late example of a topographical headpiece for a *Stationers' Almanack* featuring the Court Room at Stationers' Hall. Drawn by Hanslip Fletcher. Process probably lithotint. Published for the Stationers' Company by Cassell & Co., 1925.

leaning on the parapet of the Somerset House terrace has been replaced by a nursemaid with a pram. Below a detachment of Guards march eastwards along the Embankment.

In the 1870s, 1880s and 1890s Roberts & Leete made full use of the Godfrey family. For their 1890 view of the 'Tower of London' they used the portrait painter and banknote engraver, Louis Godfrey. Louis was the brother of Henry P. Godfrey who had engraved 'Chester', and the son of John Godfrey who drew and engraved not only 'Harrow on the Hill', but also engraved 'Milford Avon and Docks', 'Edinburgh', 'Nottingham', 'Malta' and 'Sydney'.

The golden period for the *Stationers' Almanack* headpieces was 1826 to 1890. A sizeable proportion of the great public buildings built during that period were represented by exceptionally fine steel engravings. Just a few were left out: the Hungerford Suspension Bridge,

King's Cross Station, the International Exhibition of 1862, the Natural History Museum, Holborn Viaduct and the Imperial Institute. The Natural History Museum and the Imperial Institute did feature on the *London Almanack*.

Decline

New London images continued to appear on *Stationers' Almanacks* until the mid-1890s. Then there was a spate of recycling of old plates. In 1897 the 1843 Greenwich image was reissued as 'Greenwich Hospital Fifty Years Ago', and in 1898 the 1843 Lambeth Palace image reappeared. In 1899 the 1855 Philip Phillips' 'New Bridge and Palace at Westminster' was reissued with the title 'The Houses of Parliament and Westminster Abbey'. Some adjustments had been made to the plate. The 1855 image had shown the new Westminster Bridge as it would appear on completion in 1862. The clock tower of the

Houses of Parliament was crowned with a tall, slender tower. It was never so. On the 1899 plate we see the clock tower as it was actually built. The vessels on the Thames remain the same, but the Thames-side buildings have changed. Westminster Pier has been added, and there are new buildings on the Embankment which include Norman Shaw's New Scotland Yard, built in 1888–90.

In 1895 the Stationers' Company sold off its almanack interests, including the official *Stationers' Almanack*, to the diary publishers, Charles Letts & Co. From 1896 onwards the *Stationers' Almanacks* lost their way. Steel engraving for new images was abandoned, the processes used being half-tone and photogravure. On some occasions old steel plates were reissued as historic scenes, on other occasions new topics were desperately sought. The 'Naval *Liveliness* off Gallipoli Covering the Landing of British Troops' appeared on the official almanack for 1916, for example, and 'Versailles, the Hall of Mirrors' appeared on that for 1920. Hanslip Fletcher provided a view of the Court Room at Stationers' Hall for the 1926 almanack.

Meanwhile the unofficial almanack was still just about alive. Until 1858 the firm had continued as J. & W. Robins. Then in 1864 it was listed as John Robins, and from 1865 as Brook & Roberts. In 1881 it became Roberts & Leete, who described their function as 'Wholesale and Export Stationers and Contractors, Lithographic and Letterpress Printers, Account Book Manufacturers' at 19–25 Bermondsey Street.[17] They reissued twenty-four of their plates in 1883 as an oblong folio, *English Landscape & Views Comprising Twenty-Four Engravings on Steel*, with text by J. Corbet Anderson. Like the Stationers' Company they recycled old plates. This practice became constant in the 1920s and 1930s. The firm continued to survive, it would seem, until the close of the twentieth century. In 1999 the premises of Howard Jones, Roberts & Leete Ltd in Bermondsey Street were demolished. The façade was preserved and incorporated into a new block of luxury flats called Bellway Homes.

The last *Stationers' Almanack* I have found published by Roberts & Leete is the one for 1935. It carries the steel-engraved view of Buckingham Palace that had been used exactly one hundred years earlier. The Stationers' Company's own *Stationers' Almanack* eventually became a calendar, a feeble shadow of its former self. It seems to have ceased publication in 1946, two hundred years after the publication of the first.

REFERENCES

1. Maxime Préaud, *Les Effets du Soleil: Almanachs du Règne de Louis XIV*, exhibition catalogue, Musée du Louvre, 20 January–17 April 1995.

2. See Helen Mary Petter, *The Oxford Almanacks* (Oxford: Clarendon Press, 1974).

3. Though the Stationers' Company and Guildhall Library have collections of flat-sheet *London Almanacks*, the majority of those that survive are folded.

4. See *Miniature Book News*, no. 2 (Dec. 1965), and no. 66 (Sept. 1990). The standard size was 56 × 32 mm, but some were half-size (32 mm square); some finger-size (56 × 20 mm); and a few double-size (56 × 68 mm). The standard and double-sized miniature almanacks included the engraved view, the others did not. Many of the *London Almanacks* were bound in venetian mosaic style or multi-colour moroccos. Sometimes they were of more unusual materials, such as sharkskin, mother-of-pearl or silver filigree.

5. The Stationers' Company frequently placed advertisements in London and provincial newspapers in November and December in the eighteenth century. The almanacks listed in them regularly include the *London Almanack* but never the *Stationers' Almanack*, indicating that the first was official and the second was not.

6. Since the almanacks were intended to be pinned to the wall, the designs for the headpieces included engraved frames.

7. Scatcherd's topic for the following year was 'The Death of General Montgomery', which occurred during the attack on Quebec on 31 December 1775.

8. Some of the new almanacks adopted the same titles as those published by the Stationers' Company. Carnan's *London Almanack* is an example. Advertisements placed by the Company in the *London Evening Post* and in the *York Courant* in November 1775 alerted subscribers to what Carnan was doing and instructed them to purchase only almanacks that carried the words: 'Printed for the Company of Stationers, and sold by George Hawkins at their Hall, in Ludgate-street'. That these words do not appear on either of the *Stationers' Almanack* series then being published confirms their unofficial status.

9. Presumably the Company reached a financial arrangement with Scatcherd.

10. Handlist of almanacks for 1835 at Stationers' Hall. The list includes 'The Stationers' Almanack, on royal paper, with an engraving of the King's Palace from St. James's Park'. All almanacks would be distinguished by the arms of the Company.

11. The collection of official almanacks at Stationers' Hall,

and that in the London Metropolitan Archive's Guildhall Library collection both start at 1835, the year when the stamp duty ceased to be levied.

12.   Basil Hunissett, *An Illustrated Dictionary of British Steel Engravers* (Aldershot: Scholar, 1989).

13.   J. M. W. Turner, *The Rivers of France* (London: Longman, Rees, Orme, Brown, Green & Longman, 1935–7).

14.   See Diana Brooks, *Thomas Allom (1804–1872)* (London: British Architectural Library RIBA, 1998). See also *Builder*, 9 (1851), p. 757.

15.   Charles Knight, *London* (London: Charles Knight, 1841–4), vol. 6, pp. 211–2), quoted in *Chambers' Book of Days* (London: W. & R. Chambers, 1878), pp. 715–17. Chambers also describes an earlier almanack custom: 'the Stationers' Company present annually to the Archbishop of Canterbury copies of their almanacks, which custom originated as follows: When Tenison was archbishop, a near relation of his, who was master of the Stationers' Company, thought it a compliment to call at Lambeth in the Company's stately barge, on the morning of Lord Mayor's Day [9 November], when the archbishop sent out a pint of wine for each liveryman, with bread and hot-spiced ale for the watermen and attendants; and this grew into a settled custom, the Stationers' Company acknowledging the hospitality by presenting to the archbishop a copy of the several almanacs which they publish. The wine was served in small two-handled wooden bowls, or small cups, which were provided yearly by the Company. But since the abolition of the procession by water on Lord Mayor's Day, this custom has been discontinued' (p. 14).

16.   J. F. C. Phillips, *The Shepherds in a Wider World: A Supplement to Shepherd's London* (1981).

17.   *A Descriptive Account of South London – Illustrated* (Brighton: W. T. Pike & Co. [*c*.1895?]).

THE CATALOGUE

Scope

The London headpieces described in the Catalogue begin in 1800 and continue till 1900. At this point the Stationers seem to have run out of ideas and resurrected old steel plates. Thus, for example, 'Lambeth Palace, The Residences of His Grace the Archbishop of Canterbury' (1834) reappeared on the almanacks for 1898 and 1931; 'The New Law Courts' (1880) reappeared as 'The Law Courts' on the almanack for 1904; and 'Thames Embankment from Somerset House' (1873) reappeared in 1905 as 'Thames Embankment – Thirty Years Ago'. All such restrikes are described in the catalogue under the original date.

Date (in bold)

This is the date served by the almanack, not the date of publication, which will normally have been in November or December of the previous year. Where copies of the print have been found with headings attached, the firm date can be given. In some cases dates have been firmly established, from contemporary advertisements for example. In such instances the date will be in square brackets, e.g. [1830]. If I have been almost sure of a date but have found no conclusive evidence I have used square brackets with a query, e.g. [1830?]. If an approximate date has been established from the subject of the image or, for instance, from the address used by the publisher, I have used square brackets and a *circa* sign, e.g. [*c.*1830]. Where, because of shortage of evidence, the date could be more than five years either side of the date I have supplied, then I have used square brackets, the *circa* sign, and the query, e.g. [*c.*1830?].

Artist, engraver and publisher

The details supplied on the engraving are transcribed. Should the details have been established from some other source then they appear in square brackets.

Dimensions

Height followed by width in millimetres. This is the total engraved area; in the case of a headpiece with an engraved border, the dimensions will take in the border as well.

Bibliographical note

Information such as heading text, number of copies printed, sum spent on advertising, survival of the steel plate, existence of a related watercolour.

Description

Identification of topographical detail and staffage, name of the architect responsible for the building shown with his dates, indication of why the subject was selected, comparison of how the building as shown in the print differs from the building as built, and the subsequent fate of the building.

Identification of states

This is not as precise as I would have wished, and the following shows why.

The headpieces for the *Stationers' Almanacks* were issued in several forms. The official ones were published:

1. With a heading such as 'STATIONERS' ALMANACK, 1837'; with the artist, engraver and title in the bottom margin; and with the almanack letterpress text appearing below this. For many years the arms of the Company were placed in the centre of the heading.

2. With the heading, and with the bottom margin detail, but without the almanack text. It is not that the almanack text has been trimmed off: in this state the text was never there.

3. Without the heading text, and without the almanack letterpress, but often with the arms of the Company in the centre of the top margin, and always with the bottom margin detail in place. Evidently these proofs were marketed independently. Lacking the date, they could continue to be sold for as long as there was a demand.

The rival series of *Stationers' Almanacks* were also issued in three forms:

1. With the heading, bottom margin detail, and almanack text.

2. Without the heading and almanack text, but with bottom margin details; i.e., as proofs that could be separately marketed.

3. Without heading and almanack text, and with the original text removed from the bottom

margin. The artist and engraver details are re-engraved for the bottom margin, but there is no title. In this form they were frequently printed on india paper.

More often than not, at the end of the year a purchaser of a *Stationers' Almanack* would slice off both the heading and the almanack text, retaining just the image and perhaps the lower margin details. Because of this, establishing in which form a particular *Stationers' Almanack* headpiece might have been issued initially can be impossible. This has made cataloguing difficult. Bibliographically, the proper practice would have been to restrict oneself to the minority of items which were as complete as when published, and to have distinguished clearly between them. Unfortunately, the resulting catalogue would have consisted mainly of holes. Practicability has therefore been given priority over bibliographical purity, and prints, for instance, located for State 1 in any entry may be complete with almanack, lacking the almanack, lacking heading and almanack, or lacking everything except the image. I anticipate that most users of the catalogue will not be over concerned — indeed, may never notice this bibliographical infelicity — their number one concern being to learn what images exist and where to find them.

Spelling of almanac(k)
The Stationers' official almanack used a 'k' in its spelling until 1872. The unofficial almanack, however, continued to use it until 1896. In this volume I have used the 'k', except in those later instances where the letter 'c' concludes the word on the original.

Survival of the steel plates
Many of the plates for printing the headpieces for the unofficial *Stationers' Almanack* of J. Robins & Sons, J. & W. Robins, Brook & Roberts, and Roberts & Leete, are presumed to survive. In the 1980s impressions from them were being marketed by the Islington copper-plate printers, Mauroo & Sons Ltd. The existence of these impressions is noted in the catalogue entries. I am informed that more recently the plates were acquired by the postage-stamp designer R. Granger Barrett. Where the plates are now I have been unable to discover. Perhaps someone out there will be able to tell me.

ABBREVIATIONS

Anderson	J. Corbet Anderson, *English Landscapes & Views, Comprising Twenty-Four Engravings on Steel ...* (London: Roberts & Leete, 1883)
Locations	
BL	British Library
BL-M	British Library, Map Library
BL-MSS	British Library, Manuscripts Department
BM	British Museum, Department of Prints & Drawings
BofE	Bank of England
BodL	Bodleian Library
BU	Brown University Library
CamPL	Camden Public Libraries
CUL	Cambridge University Library
GL	Guildhall Library
GrPL	Greenwich Public Libraries, Local History Collection
HarPL	Harrow Public Libraries
LMA	London Metropolitan Archives
LMA-GL	Ex-Guildhall Library items at London Metropolitan Archives
ML	Museum of London

ML-D	Museum in Docklands
NAM	National Army Museum
NMM	National Maritime Museum
P	Private collection
RL	Royal Library, Windsor
SA	*Stationers' Almanac(k)*
SC	Worshipful Company of Stationers
SofA	Society of Antiquaries
SMHSP	State Museum of the History of St Petersburg
UC	University College, London
WanPL	Wandsworth Public Libraries
Well	Wellcome Institute for the History of Medicine
WesCA	Westminster City Archives
WesCA-M	Westminster City Archives (Marylebone)
YCBA	Yale Center for British Art

*   An asterisk preceding the date indicates it is an unofficial *Stationers' Almanack*. The absence of an asterisk indicates it is an official *Stationers' Almanack*.
*   An asterisk following the date for a *London Almanack* indicates it is bound as a miniature book.

*1800

His Majesty accompanied by the Prince of Wales and the Dukes of York and Gloucester receiving the Volunteer Corps of London and its Vicinity in Hyde Park on 4th of June 1799.

London, Published Nov. 18, 1799, by I. Scatcherd, Ave Maria Lane.

230 × 440 mm

The heading reads: 'THE STATIONERS ALMANACK FOR 1800'. Lozenge-shaped image within a rectangle.

The review took place on the George III's birthday. It was reported in *The Times*, 5 June 1799:

... Precisely at nine the King, accompanied by the Prince of Wales, Dukes of York, Kent, Cumberland, and Gloucester, and attended by several General officers, Aids de Camp, and a party of Grenadiers, and the two regiments of Life Guards, entered the Park. On his Majesty's arrival a salute was fired, and the evolutions commenced according to the orders issued by the Duke of York. The troops then passed His Majesty in a line, under the direction of General Dundas, who preceded them on horseback. After which the whole number waved their military caps in the air and gave three cheers. A salute of 21 guns was then fired to conclude the Review ...

Copies seen: NAM; WesCA

*1805

The Landing of the Right Honble. the Lord Mayor Aldermen, &c. at Greenwich on May 18th 1804, on their way to Blackheath to present Colours to the Several Regiments of Loyal London Volunteers as voted to them by the Common Council of the City of London, for their Patriotic exertions to repel the attempts of Invasion by an implacable enemy.

[Edward Francis] Burney del.

Woodthorpe sculpt. 29 Fetter Lane

Published by Scatcherd & Letterman, Ave-Maria Lane, Novr. 18, 1804.

223 × 440 mm (including engraved border)

Line engraving

In top margin: 'STATIONERS ALMANACK, 1805'. The four corners of the image are occupied by acanthus leaves (symbol of triumph).

The Lord Mayor, Alderman John Perring, attended by the Duke of York and Lords Harrington and Amherst, had embarked in the City state barge at the Tower of London, and then proceeded by water to Greenwich, followed by a flotilla of 100 boats carrying the volunteers. He disembarked at the centre stairs. The volunteers then lined up and marched up Greenwich Hill to the heath of Blackheath where the Lord Mayor dedicated the colours, and delivered a patriotic speech. (For a full account of the occasion, see Neil Rhind, *The Heath* (London: Bookshop Blackheath Ltd, 2002), pp. 24–25). The Greenwich Hospital, the Royal Naval Hospital for disabled seamen, in this headpiece occupies the background.

Copies seen: BL-M; LMA-GL; GrPL; NAM; SC

Ref: No. 1855 in *Index to British Military Costume Prints* (London: Army Museums Ogilby Trust, 1972).

*[1806?]

A VIEW of the opening of the LONDON DOCKS WAPPING on the 31st of January, 1805.

[Edward Francis] Burney del.

V. Woodthorpe Sc. 29 Fetter Lane.

Published, November, 18, 1805, by Scatcherd & Letterman, Ave-Maria Lane.

217 × 435 mm (including engraved border)

Line engraving

At top left of image the arms of the Corporation of London; at top right Mercury's caduceus; at bottom left a dolphin; at bottom right a cornucopia. A note on the National Maritime Museum's copy states: 'Original Drawing by E.F. Burney is in the Ingram Collection'.

The London Dock was London's second dock, the first being the West India Dock, opened in 1802. Its engineer was John Rennie (1761–1821). Although the Corporation of London was initially hostile to this development, the Lord Mayor of London served as one of its directors. The vessel given the honour of being the first to enter the dock and be unloaded there was the *London Packet*, carrying wine from Oporto. On board were the pilot, John Rennie, and various noblemen. The engraving depicts the boat entering the great dock. Several welcoming shots are fired by ships, and spectators salute her with nine huzzas. A band (not shown) plays 'Rule Britannia'. The church in the background is St George in the East.

Copies seen: LMA-GL; ML-D; NMM

*1815

HIS ROYAL HIGHNESS, the PRINCE REGENT, accompanied by the EMPEROR of RUSSIA, the KING OF PRUSSIA, MARSHALL BLUCHER, COUNT PLATOFF, and a numerous suite of distinguished Personages receiving the Troops in Hyde Park on the 20th of June 1814, the day on which Peace was proclaimed with France.

Engraved by J. Edwards, From the Original drawing, by J. Atkinson, 1814.

215 × 415 mm

Line engraving

In top margin: 'STATIONERS ALMANACK 1815'. There is a very attractive related watercolour drawing in National Army Museum. Not listed in *Index to British Military Costume Prints* (London: Army Museums Ogilby Trust, 1972).

Following the abdication and banishment of Napoleon in April 1814, the Tsar of Russia and the King of Prussia were invited to London. A grand review of all the regular troops and most of the volunteers in and near the metropolis took place in Hyde Park on 20 June. The proclamation of peace was read at a series of

sites in Westminster and the City, finishing up at the Royal Exchange. Atkinson's view would seem to be looking east, towards Park Lane. From left to right are Platoff, the Prince Regent, Alexander, Blucher and the King of Prussia.

Copies seen: NAM; WesAC

*1818

VIEW of the SOUTHWARK BRIDGE.

Dedicated to the Right Hon. CHRISTOPHER SMITH, Lord Mayor of the City of London, by his obedient humble Servant, Catherine Ryland.

London: Printed (for the Proprietoress) by Ann Kemmish, 17 King-street, Borough.

Pubd. by C. Ryland, (late I. Ryland) 83, Cannon Street.

200 × 414 mm

Line engraving

In margin top centre: 'STATIONER'S ALMANACK for 1818'.

Southwark Bridge, like Waterloo Bridge which was under construction at the same time, was designed by John Rennie (1761–1821). It was built of cast iron (6,000 tons) and had just three arches. The ceremonial opening was held in the evening of 24 March 1819 when it was illuminated by lamps and declared open as the clock on St Paul's Cathedral struck midnight. The present bridge, designed by Sir Ernest George and constructed by Mott & Hay, replaced Rennie's bridge in 1912–21.

Ryland's crudely executed view is taken from a point above London Bridge and looks west, with Southwark on the left, the City of London on the right, and Blackfriars Bridge upstream. It has been copied from a small aquatint featured as plate 24 in volume 7 of Ackermann's *Repository of Arts* (1812). The bridge does not correspond with the bridge as built: the piers in particular are quite different.

Copies seen: LMA-GL

*[1818?]
THE CEREMONY OF OPENING WATERLOO BRIDGE, JUNE 18 1817.

Engraved by J. Edwards, from an Original Drawing by J. A. Atkinson.

215 × 426 mm (including engraved border)

Line engraving

Atkinson's pen, ink and watercolour drawing was auctioned at Sotheby's on 29 Nov. 2000. No. 2292 in *Index to British Military Costume Prints* (London: Army Museums Ogilby Trust, 1972).

When originally conceived in 1809, Waterloo Bridge was to have been called Strand Bridge, and the engineer was to have been George Dodd. In the event it was the designs of John Rennie (1761–81) that were adopted, and an Act in 1816 sanctioned the change of name to Waterloo Bridge. The bridge was opened by the Prince Regent on the second anniversary of the Battle of Waterloo, 18 June 1817. 'His Royal Highness', *The Times* reported (19 June 1817), '... walked

along the western side of the bridge between the Duke of York and the Duke of Wellington, followed by a number of military officers, officers of state, and persons of distinction, and attended by a military guard of honour'. The Prince Regent is seen in the centre of the image in military attire. The Duke of York stands on the Prince Regent's right, the Duke of Wellington on his left. The occasion was attended by the staff officers engaged in the Battle of Waterloo. The *St James's Chronicle* reported that the military wore laurels; this is to be seen in the engraving. The civilian couple on the left are probably Rennie and his wife. The clouds in the background have been created by the artillery firing salutes.

Copies seen: LMA-GL; NAM

*1819
NEW CUSTOM HOUSE, LONDON.

NEW CUSTOM HOUSE, LONDON.

London, Published by J. ROBINS & Co. Ivy Lane, Paternoster Row,

C. RYLAND, 83, Cannon Street, and J. ROBINS & SONS, No. 57 Tooley Street.

253 × 460 mm (dimensions of plate impression)

Line engraving

In top margin: 'STATIONERS ALMANACK, FOR THE YEAR 1819'. In margin top centre arms of the Corporation of London, and a non-heraldic device (representing H.M. Customs?). In left margin the seated figure of Britannia; in right margin a second female figure representing the City, seated on bale, who wears a mural crown and holds a caduceus in her left hand and a rudder in her right. There is a related pen-and-wash drawing in the London Metropolitan Archives (City CA 29318). The text for the heading that has been sketched in for the engraver reads: 'STATIONERS ALMANACK FOR THE YEAR 1818'.

The new Custom House building was designed by David Laing (1774–1856), Surveyor of

Buildings to the Board of Customs. It replaced that of Thomas Ripley, burnt down in 1814. Laing's building was completed in 1817. Eight years later the centre part of the front had to be pulled down because of subsidence, and then rebuilt by Sir Robert Smirke (1781–1867) at a cost of £200,000. Laing was suspended from office and obliged to retire from practice. In the background to the left of the Custom House is St Magnus the Martyr.

Copies seen: BM; LMA-GL; ML-D

*1820
SOUTHWARK BRIDGE.

Engraved by P. Rothwell, from an original Drawing by I. Hassell.

220 × 422 mm

Line engraving

In top margin: 'STATIONERS ALMANACK 1820'. Title and engraver's details in bottom margin. Within the image, on a floating log: 'J. Hassell 1819'. Hassell's original watercolour drawing is in the London Metropolitan Archives (formerly Guildhall Library collection).

Rennie's cast-iron Southwark Bridge (see *1818) looking east. Protruding above the bridge on the left are the Monument, St Dunstan in the East, and St Magnus the Martyr, and on the right the tower of St Saviour's is just visible. Through the arches one sees Old London Bridge, and behind it the Tower of London.

Copies seen: BM

*1821
WATERLOO BRIDGE.

W. G. Moss Del.

J. J. Shury Sculp.

197 × 416 mm

Line engraving

In top margin: 'STATIONER'S ALMANACK FOR 1821'. Below title: 'This Bridge was begun October 11th 1811, and open'd June 18th 1817, it consists of 9 Semi elliptical Arches, each of 120 feet span, and cost upwards of £1,000,000'.

Waterloo Bridge looking upstream towards Westminster from the Lambeth shore. The Italian sculptor, Antonio Canova, described Rennie's bridge as 'the noblest bridge in the world ... alone worth coming to London to see'. The building on the right with the imposing river terrace is Somerset House, which was designed by Sir William Chambers (1723–96) and built to accommodate learned societies such as the Royal Society, the Royal Academy of Arts and the Society of Antiquaries at the end of the eighteenth century.

Copies seen: BM; LMA-GL

*[1822?]
THE CORONATION of KING GEORGE the FOURTH.

Engraved by J. Chapman from a painting by J. Fussell.

190 × 416 mm

Steel engraving

The plate probably survives: modern impressions have been made from it.

The crowning ceremony in Westminster Abbey, seen from the altar. Behind is the Chair of State where the King received homage. Above are the stalls of ticket holders. To the left is the royal box, and above it the foreign ministers' box. In front of these boxes is the offering table, and next to this stands the Marquis of Salisbury with St Edward's staff. The King, clad in the royal robe of state, sits in King Edward's Chair, holding the orb in right hand and the sceptre in left. The Archbishop of Canterbury, attended by fellow bishops, is placing the crown on the monarch's head. The herald, to the front of the group on the right, would seem to be Sir George Nayler, deputy Garter on this occasion, and Garter from 1822. On the extreme right, seated bishops act as supporters. The event took place on 19 July 1821.

The image is very crude and does not begin to compare with other representations of the same occasion — those by P. Stephanhoff, for example.

State 1
Imprint: 'Published by J. Robins & Co. Ivy Lane, Paternoster Row'.

Copies seen: WesCA

State 2
In company with several other headpieces, this headpiece would seem to have been reissued in the early years of the twentieth century. The title now continues: 'FROM THE ORIGINAL PLATE ENGRAVED IN 1821'. Imprint: 'Published by Roberts & Leete, Ltd. London'.

Copies seen: LMA-GL

*1823
VIEW OF THE ROYAL EXCHANGE.

222 × 425 mm

Steel engraving?

In top margin: 'STATIONERS' ALMANACK, 1823'.

There is a related watercolour perspective for this engraving at Mercers' Hall. See *The Royal Exchange*, edited by Ann Saunders (London: London Topographical Society, 1997), pl. VIII.

This shows the south front of the second Royal Exchange, Cornhill. The building was designed by Edward Jerman (d. 1668) and erected on the site of the first Royal Exchange after the Great Fire of 1666. In 1819 Jerman's wooden tower was found to be unsafe. George Smith (1783–1869), Surveyor to the Gresham Committee, was appointed to carry out the necessary rebuilding and repairs. His new entrance front and stone tower would be completed in 1826. To the right of the entrance, on the edge of the pavement, can be seen the Cornhill pump. On the right are the premises of the Cornhill coffee-house keeper, Thomas Terry.

Copies seen: LMA; LMA-GL

*1823
HIS MAJESTY'S EMBARKATION at GREENWICH, for SCOTLAND, AUGUST 10th 1822.

Engraved by J. Chapman, from a painting by J. Fussell.

Published by J. Robins & Co. Ivy Lane, Paternoster Row.

Steel engraving?

192 × 415 mm

In top margin: 'STATIONERS ALMANACK FOR 1823'. The almanack was advertised in the *Courier*, 16 Nov. 1822, where it was described as 'taken on the spot', and priced at 3s. 6d. The plate probably survives: modern impressions have been made from it.

On 10 Aug. 1822 George IV embarked at Greenwich on his 'Northern Excursion', a state visit to Scotland. It was the first royal visit since Charles II and excited huge interest. The event was recorded by several artists. The Royal Collection, for example, has a watercolour of the occasion by Robert Havell, and the Laing Gallery, Newcastle, has another fine watercolour by Thomas Miles Richardson Senior. The comparatively crude *Stationers' Almanack* image shows the King standing in a skiff, which is being rowed by watermen in livery. He acknowledges the cheers of his subjects, as he proceeds to the royal yacht, the *Royal George* (the vessel in the centre). The royal yacht would be towed down river as far as Gravesend by the steam packet *Comet*. It would be attended by the Lord Mayor's barge, to be seen on the left, towed by the *Royal Sovereign* steamboat.

Copies seen: BL-MSS; LMA-GL

*1825

BANK OF ENGLAND.

215 × 415 mm

Steel engraving

In top margin: 'STATIONERS' ALMANACK, 1825'. No. 80 in *An Historical Catalogue of Engravings, Drawings, and Paintings in the Bank of England* (London: Bank of England, 1928).

The Bank viewed from the south, with George Sampson's centre and Sir John Soane's wings. When completed, Soane's building covered three and a half acres. The Bank, with the exception of the outer wall, would be rebuilt by Sir Herbert Baker (1925–39). On extreme right in this image is St Bartholomew-by-the-Exchange, demolished 1840–1.

Copies seen: B of E; LMA; LMA-GL

1826

VIEW IN THE REGENT'S PARK.

Drawn and engraved by Thos. Higham.

222 × 400 mm

Steel engraving

In top margin: 'STATIONERS ALMANACK, 1826'. Key to Nash terraces below image. Advertised in *The Times*, 13 Dec. 1825:

This day is published, price 3s.6d., THE STATIONERS' ALMANACK for 1926, with considerable improvements. This almanack, hitherto published by Mr. Scatcherd, but which will be continued by the Company of Stationers, is

embellished with an elegantly engraved view in the Regent's Park. And, in addition to the information that has usually been given, it contains the following useful lists: His Majesty's Ministers — The Principal Law Officers and Judges — The Commissioners and other Officers of the Board of Admiralty, Navy, Army, India Affairs, and Trade — Directors of the Bank of England, and East India Company — the Lord Mayor, Sheriffs, Aldermen, and City Officers — with a variety of useful Tables of Reference, including the most recent changes in each department. London, printed for the Company of Stationers; and sold by G. Greenhill, at their Hall, Ludgate street; and by all booksellers in the United Kingdom.

5,500 copies of this issue of the *Stationers' Almanack* were printed. Someone called Bishop was paid £28 14s. 4d. for working the plate.

Regent's Park was laid out between 1812 and 1828 to the design of John Nash (1752–1835). Grand terraces were erected around its periphery. In Higham's view, taken from the Park side of the Outer Circle and looking south-east, we see York Terrace (built 1822), Cornwall Terrace (built 1823), and Sussex Place (built 1822). The subject of the engraving, however, is Hanover Terrace (built 1822–3), which was also designed by Nash. Here at ground level he introduced an arcaded feature. Situated immediately behind Hanover Terrace is Kent Terrace, where, in a basement flat, the author of this book once briefly lived.

Copies seen: BM; LMA; LMA-G; WesCA-M

1827

VIEW OF THE NEW PUBLIC OFFICES, WHITEHALL.

T. Higham, del. et sc.

212 × 398 mm

Steel engraving

In top margin: 'STATIONERS ALMANACK FOR 1827'. 5,500 copies of this almanack were printed. For working the plate Bishop was paid £29 14s. 4d.

The new Government Offices were designed by Sir John Soane (1753–1837), erected 1824–8, and much criticized. Soane could never 'leave

out the knobs', as Sir John Summerson put it. In fact, he had been obliged to redesign it in a much richer Corinthian order by Frederick Robinson, Chancellor of the Exchequer. The building accommodated the Privy Council Office (on the Downing Street Corner), and the Board of Trade. The building on the extreme left is the Irish Office. In Downing Street, just beyond the Privy Council Office, the door of No. 10 can be identified. On the right of the image can be seen the old Tudor Home Office and Henry Holland's portico and dome for York (now Dover) House. The staffage includes various street criers, two dogs playing, and a C-sprung landau (or possibly a coach) being drawn by two pairs of postilion-driven horses.

Soane's building would be successfully remodelled by Sir Charles Barry in 1844–5 (see **1848** and ***1848**).

Copies seen: BM; LMA; LMA-GL; WesCA

*[1827?]
[THE PALACE OF WESTMINSTER AND WESTMINSTER ABBEY]

Engraved by R. Brandard, from a Drawing by A. Pugin.
Published Novr. 20 1826 by J. Robins & Sons.
190 × 410 mm
Steel engraving

Only copy seen lacks heading and title.

The view is down Margaret Street to the Houses of Parliament and Westminster Abbey, across the area which, when it was laid out by Sir Charles Barry in 1868, would become Parliament Square. Sir John Soane rebuilt the north front of Westminster Hall, 1818–20, and the new Courts alongside, 1822–5, in a neo-

classical style. He was forced to 'Gothicize' (see S. Bradley and N. Pevsner, *London 6 Westminster* (New Haven & London: Yale University Press, 2003, p. 6). Staffage includes carriages on a rank outside Westminster Hall, a crowd being addressed by an orator, a watering cart, two boxers in action spurred on by a crowd of spectators, and a liveried carriage on the right.

Copies seen: WesCA

1828
THE NEW POST OFFICE.

Thos. Higham delt. et sculp.
210 × 400 mm
Steel engraving

In t. margin: 'STATIONERS' ALMANACK FOR 1828'.

The General Post Office building, commenced in 1823 and completed in 1829, occupied the site on the east side of St Martin le Grand between St Anne's Lane (now part of Gresham Street) at the north and the junction of Newgate Street and Cheapside at the south. It was designed by Sir Robert Smirke (1781–1867). The façade was Greek Ionic. It had three handsome porticoes. The main entrance was under the central portico. This led into a Grand Public Hall which extended right across the building. On the ground floor were Inland, Foreign and Two-Penny Post Departments, and offices for wrongly addressed, returned and 'dead' letters. The Board Room, the Secretary's rooms and solicitors' offices were on the first floor, and sleeping rooms for the clerks of the Foreign Department, on the second and third floors, 'it being important, for the uncertainty of the time of arrival of the mails, that they should always be on the spot'. The building boasted a thousand argand burners; the Inland Department was 'preserved of an equable and agreeable temperature at all times by a warm-air apparatus designed by Mr Sylvester'. The building was demolished in 1913.

In the steel engraving the width of the street in front of the building is greatly exaggerated.

Copies seen: LMA; LMA-GL; ML

*[1828?]

NEW PALACE, ST. JAMES'S PARK.

Engraved by Wallis from a Drawing by A. Pugin.
Published Novr. 20 1827 by J. Robins & Sons.
194 × 397 mm
Steel engraving

There is a related, unsigned drawing for this image at the Museum of London, reproduced on p. 281 of *London — World City*, edited by Celina Fox (New Haven & London: Yale University Press, 1992). It is in pen and ink and watercolour with body colour. The watermark date is 1826. The steel plate probably survives: modern impressions have been made from it.

This view is based on the design for adapting and expanding Buckingham House which John Nash (1752–1835) produced in 1825. It lacks the Marble Arch which would provide it with a triumphal entrance (see **1835**), but shows the large cupola which was almost immediately replaced. When half-built, parts of the building were taken down and then rebuilt. The *British Almanac* for 1829 explained to its subscribers: 'The King's Palace at Pimlico is undergoing great alterations by raising the wings. These

alterations are estimated to cost £50,000, and the whole Palace £432,926. A Committee of the House of Commons expresses its dissatisfaction with these alterations, "not originally contemplated, for the purpose of rectifying a defect which scarcely could have occurred if a model of the entire edifice had previously been made and duly examined"'. Government criticism of the soaring costs led to Nash's disgrace. When the King died in 1830, the Palace was taken out of Nash's hands; a Select Committee was set up to enquire into his conduct.

The staffage includes civilian and military pedestrians, three gigs, a sociable (the open coach), a liveried coach, and troops on parade.

Augustus Charles Pugin (1762–1832), the artist responsible for drawing this headpiece, had been engaged by John Nash as an assistant back in *c*.1792, and continued working for him, on and off, for many years as his draughtsman and perspectivist. A record of the commissioning of a perspective of Buckingham Palace appears in John Nash's account book (RIBA Library). This was the last time Nash employed Pugin. (Information kindly supplied by Rosemary Hill).

Copies seen: BM; LMA-GL; ML; WesCA

1829

THE UNIVERSITY OF LONDON.

Engd. by Thos. Higham.
202 × 406 mm

Steel engraving

In top margin: 'STATIONER'S ALMANACK FOR 1829'. Below frame-line: 'From the Designs of W. Wilkins'. 5,500 copies of the almanack were printed. Adlard was paid £29 6s. 8d. for printing the headpiece.

University College was founded in 1826 so that non-Anglicans, debarred from Oxford and Cambridge, could enjoy the benefit of a university education. The building for the College was erected in Gower Street between 1827 and 1828, to designs by William Wilkins (1778–1839), architect of the National Gallery. What we see here is Wilkins' award-winning design — not the building as actually built (see *London — World City, 1800–1840* (New Haven and London: Yale University Press, 1992), pp. 565–6). When this almanack was published, only the central range with its handsome portico existed. This continued to be the situation until 1868 when the building of the lateral ranges was at last begun — but not according to Wilkins' design. The *British Almanac* for 1828 reported that the London University building was 'advancing with great rapidity', and that a large part of the building had been roofed in. In 1829 it reported that the building had been sufficiently completed 'for the commencement of the Academical Session'.

The image was probably copied from Wilkins' perspective, unlocated. (It is not amongst the original architectural drawings for the building held in the Strang Print Room, University College.)

Copies seen: CamPL; LMA; LMA-GL; ML; UC

*[1829?]
HYDE PARK CORNER.

Engraved by A. Bairns from a drawing by Schrubellie [Schnebbelie surely intended].
Published Novr. 18. 1828, by J. Robins & Sons.
195 × 404 mm
Steel engraving

Scene looking west towards Knightsbridge, the Roman 'Pimlico' Arch on the left, and the Ionic Screen on the right. Both structures were designed by Decimus Burton (1800–81). The Arch formed the entrance to Constitution Hill leading to Buckingham Palace, and thus, at this time, served the Palace as an outer gateway; the Screen formed a graceful entrance to Hyde Park. On the left, behind the Arch can be seen William Wilkins' new St George's Hospital (begun 1827), but also part of the old hospital, not yet demolished. In the centre a boy riding a donkey side-saddle, seems, despite all odds, to be more or less in control of an unlikely herd of sheep, donkeys and cows. In the background there is a travelling coach with personal servants, and a column of Grenadier Guards.

Schnebbelie's image shows the Arch as Burton intended it, with frieze and statues. In a letter to the author, 3 February 2003, Steven Brindle, English Heritage's Inspector of Ancient Monuments, writes of this image: 'At this point the Hyde Park Screen was finished so it appears exactly as it is. However, the scaffolding was still up on the arch, and Burton was in correspondence in 1828–9 with the Office of Woods and Forests and the Treasury trying to persuade them to pay for the sculptural decoration. So the artist has taken his view directly from Burton's design, though he has omitted the quadriga sculpture which appears on Burton's perspective ...'. In 1846 the Arch was made to serve as the pedestal for Wyatt's 40-ton equestrian statue of Wellington. When the much-abused statue was removed in 1888, the Arch was realigned on a new axis and its relationship to the Screen effectively destroyed.

Copies seen: P

1830
THE COLOSSEUM, REGENT'S PARK.

Drawn by E. T. Parris.
Engraved by Thos. Higham.
200 × 400 mm
Steel engraving

In top margin: 'STATIONERS' ALMANACK, 1830'. A notice of the engraving (no mention of the calendar) appeared the *Literary Gazette*, 7 Nov. 1829. 5,500 copies of the almanack were printed. For printing the headpiece Adlard was paid £29 2s. 8d.

The Colosseum, located at the south-east corner of Regent's Park, was a panorama rotunda. Designed by Decimus Burton (1800–81), it was erected in 1824–6 to house a giant 360-degree panorama of London as seen from the summit of St Paul's. This work of art had been drawn by the land surveyor, Thomas Hornor (1785–1844). It was painted by a crew of artists under the direction of Edmund Thomas Parris (the artist responsible for this image). The building was opened to the public in January 1829. It remained a prominent London landmark until its demolition in May 1875. Cambridge Gate now stands on the site.

The engraving shows the scene looking across the Outer Circle from Regent's Park. Fashionable visitors in a landau make their arrival at the North Lodge entrance. To the right of the rotunda can be seen the South Lodge, and behind it the Adult Orphan School. In the distance is Trinity Church and St Andrew's Place. The railings at the Colosseum were painted in imitation of bronze. In front of the columns were placed five American aloes. The building itself was painted in various tones of grey, yellow and brown to make it look as if it were a temple 2,000 years old. On top of the dome can be seen the Exterior Gallery with visitors enjoying the real, living panorama of London.

Copies seen: BM; CamPL; LMA-GL; ML; WesCA-M

*[1830?]

NEW LONDON BRIDGE.

Engraved by S. Rogers from a Drawing by A. Pugin.
198 × 432 mm
Steel engraving

The steel plate probably survives: modern impressions have been made from it. There is a related unsigned pencil drawing by Augustus Charles Pugin in the London Metropolitan Archives (ex-Guildhall Library).

New London Bridge looking east. Old London Bridge can be seen through the arches. A forest of masts beyond.

Royal assent for the Act for Rebuilding London Bridge was given on 4 July 1823. Designed by John Rennie (1761–1821), the new bridge was realized by his son, John Rennie Junior (1794–1874). The work took seven and a half years, and forty of the 800 men engaged to build it died in accidents. Demolition of Old London Bridge would begin after the opening of

New London Bridge in 1831, and was completed in 1832.

State 1
'Published Novr. 17, 1829, by J. Robins & Sons Tooley Street.' The bridge is prematurely represented as if construction had already finished.
Copies seen: LMA-GL

State 2
'Published Augt. 1, 1831, by J. Robins & Sons, Tooley Street.' This was the date of the royal opening of New London Bridge: evidently Robins & Sons, their works in Tooley Street being close by, were inspired to reissue the print as a souvenir. Thirteen lines of descriptive letterpress were added beneath the title. The image itself has been updated so as to show the gas lamps. It is explained that the lamp-posts had been made from cannon taken during the Napoleonic Wars.
Copies seen: LMA-GL; ML-D

State 3
Same as State 2 but without descriptive text. The modern re-strike is in this state.
Copies seen: LMA

1831

THE GARDEN FRONT OF THE KING'S PALACE, AT PIMLICO.

Drawn & Engraved by Thos. Higham.
202 × 405 mm
Steel engraving

In top margin: 'STATIONERS' ALMANACK FOR 1831'. 5,500 copies of the almanack were printed.

Higham's view of the Garden (or West) Front of Nash's Buckingham Palace (occupied at this time by William IV) in effect forms a companion to the same artist's view from St James's Park for **1835**. It shows the building as it was before Nash's successors carried out their alterations. The pavilion on the right is now the altered Queen's Gallery. Alterations carried out on the garden were as radical as those carried out on the house, the garden's formal design giving way to a natural

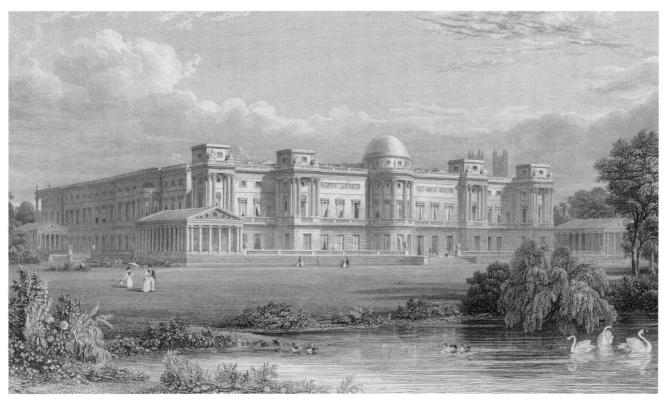

1831

one. The works were superintended by William Townsend Aiton, head gardener at Kew Gardens, though John Nash had a hand in the design, too. The lake seen in the foreground was created out of two existing pools. The earth excavated for its construction was re-utilized to become a high mound at the south side end of the garden.

Copies seen: BM; LMA; LMA-GL; ML; SMHSP

1832

NEW LONDON BRIDGE, OPENED BY HIS MAJESTY WILLIAM IV IN PERSON, AUGUST 1, 1831.

Drawn & Engraved by Thos. Higham.

202 × 400 mm

Steel engraving

In top margin: 'STATIONERS' ALMANACK FOR 1832'. 5,000 copies of the almanack were printed.

New London Bridge is viewed from the Surrey end looking upstream. St Paul's Cathedral and a segment of Southwark Bridge are visible through one of the arches.

On 1 Aug. 1831 New London Bridge was opened by William IV. He, with Queen Adelaide, arrived in a magnificent civic water procession. After a reception in a marquee erected at the northern end, the royal couple performed the ceremony of opening the bridge by walking to the southern end. There the intrepid aeronaut, Charles Green, provided a

climax by ascending in his balloon. The barge shown at the south end of the bridge is most likely the Stationers', built by Roberts in 1790.

Copies seen: BM; LMA-GL; ML-D

*[1832?]

COVENT GARDEN MARKET.

Drawn by Willm. & Fredk. J. Havell.

Engraved by Fredk. Jas. Havell.

196 × 412 mm

Steel engraving

There is a related watercolour in the British Museum (Crace XVIII 83); another related watercolour was

auctioned at Sotheby's, 17 Nov. 1983 (lot 47). A related watercolour (same one as latter?) was in the stock of The Boydell Galleries, Liverpool, in Jan. 2001.

When the Fleet Market was closed in 1826, extra demands were made on Covent Garden Market. In order to improve the facilities there, an Act of Parliament was passed in 1828, and a handsome colonnaded market building was designed by Charles Fowler (1791–1867) who would shortly afterwards design the new building for Hungerford Market. Mean and ramshackle buildings cluttering the area were rapidly swept away. The new, largely granite, building, paid for by the Duke of Bedford, was completed in 1830.

The view in the Havell engraving is taken from the east end of King Street, and we look south-east across the market, with Inigo Jones' St Paul's Church on our right. Vegetables are delivered in carts and sold from stalls; women street traders carry produce away in wicker baskets which they balance on their heads. The baskets throughout have been very closely observed: those dumped in the roadway on the left carry the initials of the Havells.

State 1
Imprint: 'Published by J. Robins & Sons, Tooley Street, Southwark'.
Copies seen: BM; LMA; LMA-GL; WesAC

State 2
In company with several other headpieces, this headpiece would seem to have been reissued in the early years of the twentieth century, its heading appropriately adjusted. The words 'IN 1827' are added to title, and the imprint reads: 'Published by Roberts & Leete, Ltd. London'.
Copies seen: LMA; LMA-GL

1833
THE DUKE OF YORK'S COLUMN. CARLTON TERRACE, ST. JAMES'S PARK.

Drawn & Engraved by Thos. Higham.

200 × 400 mm

Steel engraving

5,000 copies of the almanack were printed.

The heading on London Metropolitan Archives' copy cropped, but it appears to read: 'STATIONERS' ALMANACK, FOR 1833'.

The Duke of York, brother of George IV and heir to the throne, was Commander in Chief. The children's ditty has him pointlessly marching his ten thousand men to the top of the hill, and marching them down again. After his death in 1827 £25,000 was raised, principally by stopping a day's pay from every soldier in the British army, in order to finance the erection of this monument. The granite column, 123 feet high (37 metres), was designed by Benjamin Dean Wyatt (1775–1855), who had collaborated with the Duke in producing ambitious but abortive militaristic schemes for improving London. The bronze statue on the summit, the work of Sir Richard Westmacott (1775–1856), is so positioned that the Duke has his back to his brother's Regent Street, and is able to preside over military happenings on the Horse Guards' Parade.

Raised on the site of Carlton House, the column, actually sited in Waterloo Place, forms the focal point at the bottom of Regent Street. It was completed in 1834. Higham's engraving shows the monument as seen from St James's Park, with the Corinthian ranges of Carlton House Terrace to left and right. In the foreground women and children stroll, play, and converse. The men are chiefly soldiers in their 'number ones'. A black liveried servant in the group right of centre keeps a respectful distance. A cow sedately makes its way eastwards.

Copies seen: BM; LMA; LMA-GL; SMHSP; WesCA

*[1833?]
GREENWICH HOSPITAL.

200 × 420 mm

Steel engraving

An image consisting of the same composition and attributed to Robert Havell was auctioned at Sotheby's, 2 Mar. 1983. The catalogue entry entitled it 'The Admiral's Regatta, Greenwich', and noted the existence of a watercolour version signed by Robert Havell in the Royal Collection — no. 318 in A. P. Oppé, *English Drawings, Stuart and Georgian Periods, in the Collection of His Majesty the King at Windsor Castle* (London: Phaidon Press, 1950). A pen and ink and wash drawing, ascribed to William Havell alone, directly related to the *Stationers' Almanack* image was in the stock of MacConnal-Mason in June 1978, and was auctioned at Sotheby's, 19 Nov. 1987 (lot 128). A reduced version of the image exists. It is vignetted, and carries the words: 'Engraved for Bradshaw's Journal'. A related oil painting by Edward Pritchett was auctioned at Christie's on 24 May 2002 (lot 39). The steam vessel on the left was a regular steamboat, and the peter boat and rowing boat were shown on the right instead of the left. A crude, vignetted, plagiarized version of the image appears printed on a contemporary handkerchief, see next column.

Greenwich Hospital as seen from the north, looking across the Thames from the Isle of Dogs. On the summit of the hill behind the Hospital is Flamsteed House. To the right of the Hospital is the tower of St Mary's Church. On the river on the left a Thames paddle steamboat heads downstream. Behind it a brig sails upstream. In the foreground is a peter boat showing its wet well, and a rowing boat. In the distance in the centre lies a ceremonial barge, in a throng of wherries and other boats. In the mid-distance to the right is the Admiralty barge. On the extreme right a brig heads upstream.

The image probably represents the aftermath of William and Adelaide's Royal Aquatic Excursion on 4 May 1832. On that date the royal couple visited Woolwich Dockyard to view warships under construction (they included the *Trafalgar*), and then sailed upstream to Greenwich on the royal yacht, the *William & Mary*. 'The walk before [the Greenwich Hospital] was crowded with spectators', *The Times*, 5 May 1832, reported. After being received by the Governor, the King inspected the Painted Hall, with its naval portraits, many of them presented to the

Hospital by George IV.

State 1
'Drawn by Willm. & Fredk. Havell. Engraved by Fredk. Jas. Havell'. Imprint: 'Published by J. Robins & Sons, Tooley Street, Southwark'.
Copies seen: BL-MSS; BM; LMA; GrPL; ML; NMM

State 2
'Willm. & Fredk. J. Havell, pinx. Fredk. Jas. Havell, sculp'.
Copies seen: GrPL

State 3
Plate [17] in Anderson. Without heading, title or imprint.
Copies seen: LMA-GL; GrPL

1834

LAMBETH PALACE. THE RESIDENCE OF HIS GRACE THE ARCHBISHOP OF CANTERBURY.

Drawn & Engraved by Thos. H. Higham.

200 × 425 mm

5,000 copies of the 1834 almanack were printed.

*[**1832?**], see pp. 25–6

Lambeth Palace, begun in the early twelfth century and added to periodically, was rebuilt and restored 1828–34 by Edward Blore (1787–1879).

The *British Almanac* for 1833 announced:

The new buildings which were undertaken by the present Archbishop of Canterbury immediately after his accession to the see are just completed externally at a cost up to the present time of upwards of £55,000. These buildings stand in the gardens east of the old palace. The principal edifice is a beautiful and imposing structure. The ornamental portions are particularly rich, and have been chiefly copied from Westminster and St Alban's Abbeys ... The whole is built of Bath stone ... The library is perhaps the finest thing in the whole building.

The vehicle left of centre is a town chariot (maybe the Archbishop's), and that on the right a barouche.

The Archbishop of Canterbury was patron to the Stationers' Company. His Palace was therefore a natural and appropriate subject for *Stationers' Almanack* headpieces. The Palace also featured on the *1850 Almanack; the image for the **1834** Almanack was brought into service on two future occasions (see below).

State 1
In top margin: 'STATIONERS ALMANACK FOR 1834'.
Copies seen: BM; LMA-GL; LamPL; ML

State 2
In top margin: 'THE IMPERIAL. STATIONERS' ALMANAC FOR 1898. THE IMPERIAL'. In bottom margin of the almanack: 'Printed and Published for the Stationers' Company, London by CHARLES LETTS & CO., 3 Royal Exchange, E.C'.
Copies seen: LMA-GL

State 3
Lithographic reproduction. In top margin: 'STATIONERS' COMPANY'S [arms] ALMANAC FOR 1931'. In margin below almanack text:

'PUBLISHED BY THE WORSHIPFUL COMPANY OF STATIONERS, STATIONERS' HALL, E.C.4., AND TO BE OBTAINED FROM CHARLES LETTS & CO., SOUTHWARK BRIDGE BUILDINGS, LONDON S.E.1, OR ANY BOOKSELLER'. Priced at two shillings.
Copies seen: CUL; LMA-GL

*1834

THE POST OFFICE, ST. PAUL'S CATHEDRAL, and BULL & MOUTH INN ...

Engraved by G. J. Emblem from a Drawing by T. Allom.

202 × 406 mm

Steel engraving

The steel plate probably survives: modern impressions have been made from it. There is a related pen-and-wash drawing signed 'T. ALLOM 1833' in the London Metropolitan Archives. The Guildhall Art Gallery has a very closely related oil painting of the image signed by George Sidney Shepherd and dated 1835 (accession no. 1564).

The view is taken from a point near the north end of St Martin le Grand looking south towards Newgate Street and St Paul's. On the left is the entrance to St Anne's Lane (today part of Gresham Street). Behind the railings is the new General Post Office, designed by Sir Robert Smirke (1781–1867), and completed in 1829 (see **1828**). On the right is the entrance to the Bull & Mouth coaching inn. In the coaching age this inn was the equivalent of a major London railway terminus. A mail coach issues from the General Post Office, and a stagecoach from the Bull & Mouth. A second stagecoach and a stage wagon are arriving. The scene is one of bustle and excitement. The figures include an organ grinder with a monkey.

State 1
Title concludes with the word 'LONDON'. In top margin: 'STATIONER'S ALMANACK, 1834'. Imprint:

'Published by J. Robins & Sons, Tooley Street, London'.

Copies seen: BM; LMA; LMA-GL; ML

State 2
Word 'LONDON' removed, and imprint is: 'London, W. H. J. Carter [12, Regent Street, Pall Mall].

Copies seen: LMA- GL

State 3
Title: 'LONDON IN 1829'. Imprint: 'Published by Roberts & Leete. Ltd'.

Copies seen: P

State 4
Modern impression, without text in top margin.

Copies seen: LMA-GL

1835
THE KING'S PALACE, FROM ST. JAMES'S PARK.

Drawn & Engraved by Thos. Higham.

202 × 404 mm

Steel engraving

In the wake of the abolition of Stamp Duty, the Company issued a handbill listing the 1835 almanacks to be published on 18 Nov. 1834. The *Stationers' Almanack*, on royal paper, would carry an engraving of the King's Palace from St James's Park. It would cost 2s. (In the 1820s, both the official *Stationers' Almanack* and its rival had been priced at 3s. 6d.) In an advertisement in *The Times*, 16 Oct. 1835, the Company 'expressed their acknowledgement for the encouragement with which their endeavours to give satisfaction to the public were met last year on the occasion of the abolition of the stamp duty'. The Royal Collection has a related watercolour by Joseph Nash. In Sept. 1999 it featured in an exhibition at the Holburne Museum, Bath. Higham's version does not show the Royal Standard flying above the Marble Arch entrance, nor sheep grazing in St James's Park.

This view of the east front of Buckingham Palace forms a companion to the same artist's view of the garden front on the **1831** almanack. It seems to show Nash's projected east front rather than the front as built. From *c*.1828 Nash's triumphal arch formed a splendid entrance to the Palace. It was unceremoniously removed by Edward Blore in 1851, and re-erected at the north end of Park Lane as 'Marble Arch'.

St James's Park, formerly a formal garden with a straight canal, was transformed into a picturesque garden with a curvilinear lake and island in the late 1820s. Children amuse themselves feeding the swans.

State 1
In top margin: 'STATIONERS' [Company's arms] ALMANACK, 1835'. In bottom margin, below the almanack text: 'Chiswick: Printed by C. WHITTINGHAM, for the COMPANY OF STATIONERS; and sold by GEORGE GREENHILL, at their Hall, Ludgate-street, London'. 5,155 copies of the almanack were printed.

Copies seen: BM; LMA; LMA-GL; ML; RL; SC; SMHSP; WesAC

State 2
Lithographic reproduction. In top margin: 'STATIONERS' AND NEWSPAPER MAKERS' COMPANY'S ALMANAC FOR 1935'. In margin below almanack text: 'PUBLISHED BY THE WORSHIPFUL COMPANY OF STATIONERS, STATIONERS' HALL, E.C.4, AND TO BE OBTAINED FROM CHARLES LETTS & CO., SOUTHWARK BRIDGE BUILDINGS, LONDON S.E.1, OR ANY BOOKSELLER'. Priced at 2s.

Copies seen: CUL; LMA-GL

*[1835?]
GOLDSMITHS' HALL.

Engraved by J. Rogers, Finchley, from a Drawing by Tho. H. Shepherd.

Published by J. Robins & Sons, Tooley Street, Southwark.

195 × 412 mm

Steel engraving

The steel plate probably survives: modern impressions have been made from it.

Foster Lane had been the site of a sequence of halls of the Goldsmiths' Company since the fourteenth century. Nicholas Stone's hall, built in *c*.1634–6 and restored by Edward Jerman after the Great Fire, gave place to that of Philip Hardwick (1792–1870), which was begun in 1829 and completed in 1835. This view of Hardwick's building, with its six attached Corinthian columns, would appear to have been taken from the corner of St Anne's Lane and Noble Street, with the

entrance to Maiden Lane on the left and the entrance to Carey Lane on the right. Some of the blocks used in its construction were said to have weighed in excess of 12 tons. Perhaps it is one such block that is being drawn in the stonemason's truck down Maiden Lane. The church at the south end of Foster Lane is St Vedast; a gentleman's town coach emerges from that street. On the extreme right can be seen the wall of the new General Post Office. The image represents a stretch version of T. H. Shepherd's view of Goldsmiths' Hall for *London and its Environs in the Nineteenth Century* (London: Jones & Co., 1829–31), pl. 53.

Copies seen: BM; LMA; LMA-GL; ML

1836

ENTRANCE INTO THE CITY, BY LONDON BRIDGE.

Drawn & Engraved by Thos. Higham.

202 × 402 mm

Steel engraving

At the north end of London Bridge, and on the west side of it, is Fishmongers' Hall, designed by Henry Roberts (1803–76) and completed in 1834. Because of the height of the bridge, the building was provided with a deep substructure. An arcade, supporting a terrace, concealed the entrance to a fire-proofed warehouse extending under the building. The structure rising above it was of the Grecian Ionic order. The principal entrance was in Adelaide Place, that is, opposite the Adelaide Hotel. The water steps, to the right of the building, came into their own on ceremonial occasions. It was here, for instance, that William IV disembarked in great state for the opening of the bridge in 1831; the stairs

were frequently used by the City Fathers when embarking for the Lord Mayor's Day river procession.

To the west of Fishmongers' Hall is 'Wooding's Shades' (Simon Wooding's wine rooms), and on the opposite side of Adelaide Place is the Adelaide Hotel, a building 'well calculated for strangers that arrive in England by the steam vessels, as they will be enabled to land on a broad esplanade' (Nathaniel Whittock, *New Picture of London*, 1836).

Guests view the scene from the terrace. The Monument looms up behind it. The churches from left to right are St Swithin, St Michael Cornhill, St Magnus-the-Martyr, and St Margaret Pattens. A couple cross the bridge in a Tilbury gig. A large and heavy basket of pot plants is being balanced on the parapet of the bridge. Next to it is an exhausted woman who takes a rest. Her head gear is designed for carrying, but can she possibly have been carrying this basket?

State 1
In top margin: 'STATIONERS' [Company's arms] ALMANACK, 1836'. In bottom margin, below almanack text: 'Chiswick: Printed by C. WHITTINGHAM, for the COMPANY OF STATIONERS; and sold by GEORGE GREENHILL, at their Hall, Ludgate-street, London'. 5,500 copies of the almanack were printed.

Copies seen: BM; LMA; LMA-GL; ML; SC; SMHSP

State 2
Lithographic reproduction of State 1. In top margin: 'STATIONERS' COMPANY'S ALMANAC FOR 1928'. In margin below the almanack text: 'PUBLISHED BY THE WORSHIPFUL COMPANY OF STATIONERS, STATIONERS' HALL, E.C.4, AND TO BE OBTAINED FROM MESSRS. THOMAS DE LA RUE & COMPANY, LIMITED, OR ANY BOOKSELLER. REGISTERED AT STATIONERS' HALL'.

Copies seen: CUL; LMA-GL

*1836

BRITISH MUSEUM. GRAND CENTRAL AND EGYPTIAN SALOONS.

Engraved by Sands from a Drawing by Allom.

202 × 406 mm

Steel engraving

In top margin: 'STATIONER'S AMANACK, 1836'. The steel plate probably survives but in poor condition; I have seen no modern re strikes.

The scene is the Lower Egyptian Gallery (Room 25 of the British Museum). F. Barker and P. Jackson in *London: 2000 Years of a City and its People* (London: Cassell, 1974), p. 303, identify the exhibits as the granite lions from Nubia of 1400 BC, presented to the museum in 1835; the twin obelisks, 350 BC, gifts of George III; and in the distance the colossal head of King Thothmes, 1500 BC, discovered at Karnak by Belzoni.

State 1
Imprint: 'Published by J. Robins and Sons, Tooley Street, London'.

Copies seen: BL-M; BM; CamPL; LMA; SMHSP

State 2
Imprint below image plate impression: 'W.H.J. Carter, 12, Regent Street, Pall Mall'.

Copies seen: LMA-GL

State 3
A state with Roberts & Leete's imprint most probably existed but no copy seen.

1837

PROPOSED NEW HOUSES OF PARLIAMENT. FROM THE DESIGN OF CHARLES BARRY ESQVIRE.

Engraved by Thos. Higham.

200 × 406 mm

Steel engraving

In top margin: 'STATIONERS' [Company's arms] ALMANACK, 1837'. In bottom margin, below

almanack text: 'Chiswick: Printed by C. WHITTINGHAM, for the COMPANY OF STATIONERS; and sold by GEORGE GREENHILL, at their Hall, Ludgate-street, London'. 6,475 copies of the almanack were printed. An advertisement in *The Times*, 15 Oct. 1836, and the *Athenaeum*, 22 Oct. 1836, reads:

The Stationers Almanack for 1837 will be published on 22 November, price 2s. This Almanack, printed on a large sheet of fine royal paper will have as its embellishment a superb Engraving, by Higham, of the New Houses of Parliament, taken, by permission, from Mr. Barry's adopted Designs.

In other words the engraving was based, not on Barry's winning competition design, drawn by A. W. N. Pugin in 1835, but on the design approved by Parliament in 1836.

The river front of the proposed Houses of Parliament is shown from the south-east. This early design lacks the pitched iron roofs and a central tower added in the 1840s for a ventilating system; the Clock Tower is more slender than that which was built. Westminster Abbey is visible in the background on the left, and Labelye's Westminster Bridge is shown on the right. The artist diplomatically shows the Stationers' own state barge positioned alongside the wide flight of ceremonial stairs on the left. In the street by the King's (Victoria) Tower an event of some importance seems to be taking place: there are crowds in the street, and people look from the Abingdon Street windows. Could it be King William arriving at, or leaving, the Royal Entrance?

When Higham prepared his drawing for the 1838 almanack, construction work had not even begun. The building was completed twenty-three years later — without the ceremonial stairs.

Copies seen: BM; LMA; LMA-GL; RL; SC; SMHSP

1836, see p. 32

*1837

WINDSOR CASTLE

Engraved by Sands from a Drawing by Allom.

Published by J. Robins & Sons, Tooley Street, London.

200 × 406 mm

Steel engraving

In top margin: 'STATIONER'S ALMANACK, 1837'. The steel plate probably survives: modern impressions have been made from it. Related drawing, in pencil with brown washes heightened with white, auctioned at Christie's, 16 Nov. 1982 (lot 158). Another related drawing, with a broader format, but also in pencil with brown washes, auctioned at Sotheby's, 24 Nov. 1977 (lot 87). The print is listed as No. 2496 in the *Index to British Military Costume Prints* (London: Army Museums Ogilby Trust, 1972). The same work lists as No. 2497 what it describes as 'another impression' (in fact a copy?), engraved for the *New York Albion*, 1 Aug. 1841, by A. L. Dick.

Mounted Dragoons or Dragoon Guards ride into the Castle grounds at Castle Hill. The Henry VIII Gateway is to be seen on the left.

Copies seen: BM; SMHSP

*[c.1837?]

THE NATIONAL GALLERY — CHARING CROSS, FROM THE DESIGN OF S. *[sic]* WILKINS ESQRE. ARCHITECT.

Engraved by Sands, from a Drawing by Allom.

Harrison, Builder.

Published by J. Robins & Sons, Tooley Street, London.

200 × 410 mm

Steel engraving

The Museum of London has a copy in oils of this image signed Thomas Waters, reproduced in *London in Paint*, by Mireille Galinou and John Hayes

(London: Museum of London, 1996), p. 522. A greatly reduced copy of Allom's image features on the back-board of an anonymous paper peep-show with the title 'London' in the Jacqueline & Jonathan Gestetner Collection.

The National Gallery, erected on the site of the Royal Mews 1832–8, was designed by William Wilkins (1778–1839). Contemporaries did not care for it: the entablature was too plain, the pediment too low, and the tympanum too bare. The building not only housed the national collection, but also the Royal Academy of Arts. In its new quarters, the Royal Academy found it had less hanging space than it had had at Somerset House.

At this date the site for Trafalgar Square was cleared. The engraving, however, shows it as if built according to the proposals put forward by Wilkins in 1837. The area, he suggested, should be levelled and a terrace created to support the road immediately in front of the Gallery. A very modest naval monument forms part of his design. After Wilkins' death in 1839, Charles Barry took charge of the layout. He retained Wilkins' idea of a terrace but added statues and two fountains. A competition was held for the naval monument (see **1842**).

The building on the left is the Union Club House, designed by Sir Robert Smirke (1781–1867). On the east side of the Square can be seen the church of St-Martin-in-the-Fields, and also Morley's Hotel, built in 1831, and adapted to become South Africa House in 1921. The staffage includes a gentleman's town coach (on left), a barouche (left of centre), a troop of Horse Guards who advance from the right, a peg-legged crossing sweeper, two men who step out arm in arm, two ladies selling brushes and a man who displays a board advertising this print's engraver: 'SANDS ENGRAVER SPRING GARDENS'. (The view is taken from Spring Gardens.)

Copies seen: LMA-GL; ML; WesAC

1838

VIEW OF THE ARCHITECTURAL
IMPROVEMENTS, IN THE VICINITY OF THE
BANK, AND THE MANSION HOUSE. THE
PROPOSED SITE FOR THE WELLINGTON
MONUMENT.

Drawn & Engraved by Thos. Higham.

202 × 410 mm

Steel engraving

The view is taken from Prince's Street looking
south-east. On the left is the corner of the Bank
of England, and the west end of Threadneedle
Street. The next street is Cornhill with the
recently erected Globe Insurance building, and
then Lombard Street with St Mary Woolnoth.
Stretching into the distance is King William
Street. On the right is the front façade of the
Mansion House, its attic storey, the 'Mayor's
Nest', still in place. This would be removed in
1842. On the extreme right is the doorway to
the shop of Mrs Louisa Heppel, fruiterer.

The architectural improvement in the City
followed the line of the approach road to New
London Bridge. It extended from the City Road
in Finsbury, down Moorgate Street and Prince's
Street, and then down King William Street to
the bridge itself. Contemporaries compared the
improvement with Regent Street, constructed in
the previous decade. A statue of King William
IV was erected at the east end of King William
Street, and it was proposed that a monument to
the Duke of Wellington, who had promoted the
London Bridge Approaches Act, should be
erected at the west end (see *1838).

The staffage on this print is more spirited
than on almost any other almanack. It includes
a man who advertises a public meeting at the
Mansion House, delivery boys, omnibuses, a
boulnoir back-door cab (left of centre), a
delivery van with canvas tilt (on right), street
traders, and observers of the hectic scene who
stand on the terrace of the Mansion House.

State 1
Steel engraving. In top margin: 'STATIONERS'
[Company's arms] ALMANACK, 1838'. In bottom
margin, below almanack text: 'Chiswick: Printed by
C. WHITTINGHAM, for the COMPANY OF
STATIONERS; and sold by GEORGE GREENHILL,
at their Hall, Ludgate-street, London'. 5,900 copies
of this state of the almanack were printed.

Copies seen: BM; LMA; LMA-GL (proof); RL; SC;
Well

State 2
Lithographic reproduction. In top margin:
'STATIONERS' COMPANY'S [arms] ALMANAC
FOR 1933'. In margin below almanack text:
'PUBLISHED BY THE WORSHIPFUL COMPANY
OF STATIONERS, STATIONERS' HALL, E.C.4.,
AND TO BE OBTAINED FROM CHARLES
LETTS & CO., SOUTHWARK BRIDGE
BUILDINGS, LONDON S.E.1, OR ANY
BOOKSELLER ...'. Priced at 2s.

Copies seen: LMA-GL

*1838

THE BANK OF ENGLAND, & ROYAL
EXCHANGE, CORNHILL, WITH KING
WILLIAM STREET, the New Approach to
London Bridge, and the Site of the intended
Statue of the Duke of Wellington, near the
Mansion House. LONDON.

Drawn by J. H. Nixon.

Engraved by Henry Wallis.

Published by J. & W. Robins, 57 Tooley Street,
London.

200 × 412 mm

Steel engraving

In top margin: 'STATIONERS' ALMANACK, 1838'.
The steel plate probably survives: modern impressions
have been made from it. There is a related signed
drawing, in pen and ink and body colour, in the
London Metropolitan Archives.

On the left is Threadneedle Street with the
Bank of England, St Bartholomew-by-the-

Exchange (demolished 1840–1), and the north end of the second Royal Exchange (destroyed in a fire only a few weeks after the publication of this print). The Bank was the terminus for Schillibeer's omnibuses, and four pre-knifeboard, single-deck buses are shown parked here. The next street is Cornhill with the south end of the Royal Exchange on the left, and St Peter Cornhill and St Michael Cornhill on the right. Behind the proposed statue is the Globe Insurance Company. On the right is Lombard Street with St Mary Woolnoth, and beyond it stretches King William Street, with the tower of St Clement Eastcheap and (above the rooftops in the far distance) the Monument.

Staffage includes porters carrying bales on their heads, a policeman holding up traffic to allow pedestrians to cross, boys with a hand-drawn luggage cart, a hackney cabriolet (images of this vehicle are exceedingly rare), a short-distance stagecoach, an orange-seller, four men with advertising notices, and a stage wagon making for London Bridge and the country.

The City's Court of Common Council in 19 July 1838 voted £500 towards the expense of erecting a Wellington monument at the west end of King William Street. An equestrian statue of the Duke is shown in front of Philip Hardwick's just-completed, bow-fronted Globe Fire & Life Insurance Office. In the event a Wellington statue (not this one, but one by Chantry) would be put up in 1844 in the space cleared in front of the William Tite's new (third) Royal Exchange.

State 1
In top margin: 'STATIONER'S ALMANACK, 1838'. At bottom right of almanack text: 'SOUTHWARK.– Printed and Published by J. & W. ROBINS, Tooley-street'.
Copies seen: BM; LMA; LMA-GL; RL

State 2
[Plate re-issued on a *Stationers' Almanack* in the early years of the twentieth century. The words 'the New Approach ...' removed and replaced by: 'LONDON IN 1840'. Imprint: 'Published by Robert & Leete Ltd. London'.
Copies seen: P

State 3
Modern impression, without text in t. margin.
Copies seen: LMA-GL

1839

HYDE PARK GARDENS. FROM THE VICTORIA GATE, HYDE PARK.

From the Design of John Crake, Esq.
Drawn & Engraved by Thos. Higham.
202 × 414 mm
Steel engraving

In top margin: 'STATIONERS' [Company's arms] ALMANACK, 1839'. In bottom margin, below almanack text: 'Printed by C. WHITTINGHAM, for the COMPANY OF STATIONERS; and sold by GEORGE GREENHILL, at their Hall, Ludgate-street, London'. 6,490 copies of the almanack were printed.

John Crake (*c.*1811–59), a pupil of Decimus Burton (1800–81), designed this terrace of houses, set back on the north side of Hyde Park, in 1836. In the foreground is the Victoria Gate with a lodge, designed by Decimus Burton, 1838.
Copies seen: BM; LMA-GL; ML; RL; SC; SMHSP; WesCA-M

*1839

PORT OF LONDON. The Custom House and Buildings looking West.

Drawn by T. Allom.
Engraved by F. J. Havell.
Published by J. & W. Robins, 57, Tooley Street, London.
200 × 406 mm
Steel engraving

Companion to the *1842 almanack, 'LONDON From Somerset House looking East'. The steel plate probably survives: modern impressions have been made from it. Allom's related drawing (pencil and brown wash, heightened with white) is in the Print Room of the Victoria & Albert Museum (P.120-1920). There is a related oil painting by Allom in the Port of London Authority's collection, signed and dated on boat on left, 'ALLOM 1839'.

On the right is the Custom House, designed by David Laing (1774–1856) and built in 1813–17. The centre section was rebuilt by Sir Robert Smirke (1781–1867) in the 1820s. The Monument, and the spires of St Dunstan-in-the-East, and St Margaret Pattens can be seen

behind it. Immediately beyond the Custom House is Billingsgate Market, and then St Magnus the Martyr, the Adelaide Hotel, and Fishmongers' Hall, with St Paul's Cathedral behind. The bridges are New London Bridge, with Southwark Bridge beyond. One of the two steamboats shown on the Thames in the centre of the image is the *Boulogne* packet.

State 1
Title as above. In top margin: 'STATIONERS' ALMANACK 1839'. At bottom right of almanack text: 'SOUTHWARK.– Printed and Published by J. & W. ROBINS, Tooley-street'.

Copies seen: BM; LMA-GL; LMA; ML; ML-D; NMM; RL; SMHSP

State 2
In top margin: 'STATIONERS' ALMANAC, 1908'. Title: 'PORT OF LONDON IN 1839'. Imprint below image now: 'Published by Roberts & Leete, Ltd. London'. At bottom right in almanack text: 'LONDON Printed and Published by ROBERTS & LEETE, LTD., London S.E'.

Copies seen: GL; ML-D; YCBA

State 3
Modern impression, without text in top margin.

Copies seen: LMA-GL; ML-D

1840

VIEW OF THE REFORM CLUB HOUSE IN PALL MALL, NOW BUILDING BY CHARLES BARRY, ARCHITECT.

Drawn by G. Moore.

Engraved by Thos. Higham.

213 × 400 mm

Steel engraving

In top margin: 'STATIONERS' [Company's arms] ALMANACK, 1840'. In bottom margin, below almanack text: 'Chiswick: Printed by C. WHITTINGHAM, for the COMPANY OF STATIONERS; and sold by GEORGE GREENHILL, at their Hall, Ludgate-street, London'. 5,987 copies of the almanack were printed. The almanack sold for 2s. (see *The Times* advertisement, 25 Oct. 1839). A related drawing was auctioned at Sotheby's, 15 July 1976 (lot 42); exhibited by Appleby at Park Lane Hotel Watercolours Fair, Jan. 1986; and acquired by the Reform Club, 1986.

The Reform Club was founded in 1836 by Edward 'Bear' Ellice, Member of Parliament for Coventry and Whig party whip at the time of the Reform Bill. An architectural competition was held for the building. Seven architects entered, and Sir Charles Barry (1795–1860), who had already designed the Travellers' Club in Pall Mall, won. The Italianate Reform Club House was opened in March 1841. Moore's view of Pall Mall for the 1840 almanack, must have been drawn in 1839 or earlier, that is, before the completion of the building; presumably it was taken from the architect's perspective. Thomas Shotter Boys' lithograph for *London As It Is* (London: T. Boys, 1842) is taken from precisely the same spot as Moore's, and so, too, is George Sidney Shepherd's lithograph of 1851. Advancing eastwards down Pall Mall, the Carlton Club with people on the balcony, the Reform Club, the Travellers' Club, the Athenaeum, the United Services Club, and the Royal College of Physicians (see F. Barker and P. Jackson, *London: 2000 Years of a City and its People* (London: Cassell, 1974), p. 332) can all be identified. At the end of the street can be glimpsed Trafalgar Square, with the National Gallery, St Martin-in-the-Fields, and (in anticipation) Nelson on top of Railton's column. The vehicles in the centre of the image can be identified as a gentleman's town coach, a barouche, a cabriolet, and a second barouche.

Copies seen: BM; LMA-GL; RC; RL; SC; WesCA

*1840

HAMPTON COURT PALACE

202 × 406 mm

Steel engraving

Appears in Anderson as plate [19]. The steel plate probably survives: modern impressions have been made from it. No. 487 in B. Gascoigne and J. Ditchburn, *Images of Twickenham* (Richmond-upon-Thames: St Helena Press, 1981).

Hampton Court was abandoned as a regular royal residence in 1737, and as an occupiable royal place in 1760. In 1838, just one year after her accession, Queen Victoria abolished

admission charges and the palace immediately became a favourite place for family outings. 115,000 people visited it in 1839, and 180,000 in 1840. This view shows the east front, designed by Sir Christopher Wren (1632–1723), built between 1689 and 1694, with a small part of Wolsey's building on the right. The palace is viewed from the Great Fountain Garden. A vignetted copy of this headpiece, *Hampton Court Palace/Le Palais de Hampton Court*, was later published by J. T. Wood.

State 1
In top margin: 'STATIONERS' ALMANACK 1840'. Below image on left: 'Drawn by T. Allom', and on right: 'Engraved by T. A. Prior'. Imprint: 'Published by J. & W. Robins, 57, Tooley Street, London'. At bottom right. of almanack text: 'SOUTHWARK: – Printed & Published by J. & W. ROBINS, Tooley-street'.

Copies seen: RL; SofA

State 2
'Allom, pinx. T.A. Prior, sculp'.

Copies seen: LMA-GL

State 3
Modern impression. No title, artist, or engraver.

Copies seen: LMA-GL

1841

SOUTH WEST VIEW OF THE NEW ROYAL EXCHANGE, WILLIAM TITE, F.R.S. F.G.S. ARCHITECT.

Drawn by G. B. Moore.

Engd. by Thos. Higham.

210 × 410 mm

Steel engraving

In top margin: 'STATIONERS' [Company's arms] ALMANACK, 1841'. In bottom margin, below almanack text: 'Chiswick: Printed by C. WHITTINGHAM, for the COMPANY OF STATIONERS; and sold by GEORGE GREENHILL, at their Hall, Ludgate-street, London'. 6,674 copies of the almanack were printed.

The design by Sir William Tite (1798–1873) for the third Royal Exchange, as if viewed from the west end of Cornhill. Since the building was not completed for another three years, it must have been based on the architect's perspective. The Royal Exchange as built was in several ways an improvement on the design shown here. It had double columns, for example, and the pediment was enriched by a relievo sculptured by Westmacott. Beneath this an inscription was carved: 'ANN ELIZABETHAE R. XIII CONDITUM ANNO VICTORIAE R. VIII RESTAURATUM'. No inscription appeared on the south façade; no urns were placed on the roof.

The building on the left is the Bank of England. The vehicles from left to right consist of a landau, a stagecoach, a phaeton, a town coach, and an omnibus.

Copies seen: LMA; LMA-G; ML; SC; Well

*1841

WINDSOR CASTLE — EAST TERRACE. THE QUEEN'S PRIVATE APARTMENTS.

Drawn by T. Allom.
Engraved by T. A. Prior.
Published by J. & W. Robins, 57, Tooley Street, London.
203 × 400 mm
Steel engraving

Allom's drawing (brown washes over pencil heightened with touches of white and with scratching out) was auctioned at Sotheby's, 14 Apr. 1994 (lot 523). It was described in the catalogue as 'Queen Victoria and the Prince Consort Attended by Members of their Staff and Household on the Terrace at Windsor Castle'. The same drawing was auctioned at Christie's, 11 Nov. 1997 (lot 109). The note in the catalogue stated that it was engraved by Sands and published by J. Robins & Sons, London. The steel plate probably survives: modern impressions have been made from it. Henry Potts, dealer in Northumberland, tells me the image was used on a plate which was exhibited at the Great Exhibition.

State 1
In top margin: 'STATIONER'S ALMANACK, 1841'.
Copies seen: BM; SMHSP

State 2
Modern impression. No text in top margin.
Copies seen: P

1842

THE NELSON COLUMN, W. RAILTON, ESQR. F.G.S. ARCHITECT, WITH THE IMPROVEMENTS OF TRAFALGAR SQUARE.

Drawn by G. Moore.
Engraved by Thos. Higham.
212 × 405 mm
Steel engraving

In top margin: 'STATIONERS' [Company's arms] ALMANACK, 1842'. In bottom margin, below almanack text: 'Chiswick: Printed by C. WHITTINGHAM, and sold by GEORGE

GREENHILL, for the COMPANY OF STATIONERS, at their Hall, Ludgate-street, London'. A related drawing, in pencil and watercolour heightened by white, signed and dated '41', was auctioned at Christie's 5 March 1974 (lot 185). 6,668 copies of the almanack were printed.

An advertisement in *The Times*, 22 Dec. 1841, reads: 'Just published on a large royal sheet, price 2s., THE STATIONERS ALMANACK for 1842, embellished with a beautiful view of the Nelson Pillar, erecting by William Railton Esq., architect, &c. in Trafalgar-square, and of the improvements about to be made in the site of the square ... Proof impressions of the plate are taken off on large paper, and sold at 3s. each'.

In 1842 the walls and balustrades for Trafalgar Square were complete, but the greater part of the Square remained hidden by hoardings. The purpose of this print seems to have been to satisfy public curiosity and give Londoners an idea of how the Square might look when finished. The winning design in the Naval Monument competition was that of Willaim Railton (c.1801–77). E. H. Baily's statue of Nelson was hauled into place on top of the column in 1843; the construction of the Square was completed in the following year. Landseer's lions, however, were not put into position until 1867. Can that be a political demonstration passing the National Gallery?

The building on the left is the Union Club House, and the building in the background the National Gallery. On the east side of the Square can be seen the church of St Martin-in-the-Fields and Morley's Hotel. The Strand stretches into the distance on the right. The fountains, statuary, and (obelisk) lamps differ from those that materialized.

Copies seen: BM; LMA; LMA-G; RL; SC; SMHSP; WesCA

*1842

LONDON From Somerset House, looking East.

Drawn by T. Allom.

Engraved by T. A. Prior.

Published by J. & W. Robins, 57, Tooley Street,
London.

202 × 403 mm

Steel engraving

In top margin: 'STATIONER'S ALMANACK, 1842'.
At bottom right of almanack text: 'SOUTHWARK:–
Printed & Published by J. & W. ROBINS, Tooley-
street'. Companion to the *1839 almanack, 'PORT OF
LONDON. The Custom House and Buildings looking
West'. Allom's related drawing (pencil with brown
wash heightened with white) is in the Print Room of
the Victoria & Albert Museum (P119-1920). The steel
plate probably survives, but in poor condition: no
modern impressions have been marketed.

The view, in fact, is from the north end of
Waterloo Bridge. The first Somerset House was
built for the Lord Protector Somerset in 1547–
50. It became the palace of several queen
consorts. In the 1770 it was demolished, and on
the site arose its replacement, designed by Sir
William Chambers (1723–96). The new building
served as the home of the Royal Academy of
Arts, the Society of Antiquaries, and of several
other learned societies. It also housed various
government departments. In 1835 Sir James
Pennethorne (1801–71) provided it with a new
west wing, and Sir Robert Smirke (1781–1867)
with a new east wing, and it is in this state that
we see it here. The building was robbed of much
of its grandeur when the Victoria Embankment,
built 1864–70, severed it from the Thames.

   In Allom's view we look east towards the
City, with the spire of St Bride's, Temple
Gardens, and St Paul's in the centre, and
Blackfriars Bridge extending southwards to
Lambeth on the right. Vessels on the Thames
include a dredger, a sailed vessel, and, just
beneath us, a steamboat, onto which passengers
are embarking from Waterloo Pier.

Copies seen: BM; LMA; LMA-GL; NMM; SMHSP

1843

THE ROYAL NAVAL HOSPITAL, AT
GREENWICH.

Drawn by G. Moore.

206 × 412 mm

State 1

In top margin: 'STATIONERS' [Company's arms]
ALMANACK, 1843'. Beneath image at bottom
right: 'Engraved by Thos. Higham'. In bottom
margin, below the almanack text: 'Chiswick: Printed
by C. WHITTINGHAM, for the COMPANY OF
STATIONERS; and sold by GEORGE GREENHILL,
at their Hall, Ludgate-street, London'. 5,661 copies
of the almanack were printed.

Copies seen: BL-MSS; BM; GrPL; LMA-GL; NMM;
RL; SC

State 2

Title: 'GREENWICH HOSPITAL FIFTY YEARS
AGO'. In top margin: 'STATIONERS' COMPANY'S
[arms] ALMANAC FOR 1897'. Higham's details
removed. In bottom margin, below almanack text:
'Printed and Published for the Stationers' Company,
London, by CHARLES LETTS & CO., 3 Royal
Exchange, E.C'. Letts took over the publication of
the *Stationers' Almanack* in 1896, so this was their
first. They advertised it in the *British Almanac* for
1897: 'Price 2s., or in an Oak renewable frame, 5s.
Price of Engraving only, 3s.; or on India paper, 5s'.

Copies seen: LMA-GL

1844

SOUTH EAST VIEW OF THE NEW HALL
AND LIBRARY, LINCOLN'S INN.

PHILIP HARDWICK, ESQ. R.A. ARCHITECT.

Drawn by G. Moore.

Engraved by Thos. Higham.

205 × 406 mm

Steel engraving

In top margin: 'STATIONERS [Company's arms] ALMANACK, 1844'. In bottom margin, below almanack text: 'Chiswick: Printed for C. WHITTINGHAM, for the COMPANY OF STATIONERS; and sold by GEORGE GREENHILL, at their Hall, Ludgate-street, London'. For engraving the plate Higham was paid £8 8s. 0d. 5,599 copies of the almanack were printed.

The new Great Hall and Library at Lincoln's Inn was designed by Philip Hardwick (1792–1870). His watercolour perspective for the proposed building, dated 1842 and showing the building from the south-east, is still preserved in the Lincoln's Inn Library. It would seem to be the prototype for a steel-engraved vignette issued by J. Shury, for another steel-engraved vignette issued by Rock & Co., for the steel-engraved view by Albutt after Read in *Mighty London* (1851–5), and for this *Stationers' Almanack* view. All these views show the building as originally intended by the architect, without the terrace which appears in the illustrated account of the opening in the *Illustrated London News*, 1 Nov. 1845. The Library — the building on the right — was extended eastwards by three bays in 1872.

The first stone was laid on 20 Apr. 1843. Queen Victoria would open the building on 30 Oct. 1845.

Copies seen: BM; LMA; LMA-GL; RL; SC

*1844

LONDON FROM GREENWICH PARK.

[William Havell del.]

Engraved by T. A. Prior.

200 × 400 mm

Steel engraving

Related drawing (pencil and sepia wash heightened with white) confidently attributed to William Havell in 112th Annual Exhibition of Watercolours and Drawings at Thomas Agnew's, 1985 (no. 90 in

catalogue). It had been acquired from Miss Joyce Havell, a descendant of the artist. The steel plate probably survives: modern impressions have been made from it.

The print consists of the view from Greenwich Hill, with the Royal Observatory on the left, Greenwich Hospital in the mid-distance, and London beyond. The scene is almost certainly that on Whit Monday when Londoners traditionally took themselves to Greenwich Park. A Greenwich pensioner supplements his pocket money by charging for a peep down his telescope. A line of young ladies make their way up the hill. Once at the top they will link hands and propel themselves down the steep slope, a sport known locally as 'tumbling'.

State 1
In top margin: 'STATIONER'S ALMANACK, 1844'. At bottom right in almanack detail: 'SOUTHWARK: – Printed & Published by J. & W. ROBINS, Tooley-street'.

Copies seen: BL-MS; BM; LMA-GL; NMM; RL; SC

State 2
'Published by J. & W. Robins, 57, Tooley Street, London'.

Copies seen: BM; GrPL; NMM

State 3
Modern impression.

Copies seen: LMA-GL; NMM

1845

THE LONDON TERMINUS OF THE BRIGHTON AND DOVER RAILROADS.

Drawn by J. Marchant.

Engraved by H. Adlard.

220.5 × 405 mm

Steel engraving

In top margin: 'STATIONERS' [Company's arms] ALMANACK, 1845'. In bottom margin, below almanack text: 'Chiswick: Printed by C.

WHITTINGHAM, for the COMPANY OF STATIONERS; and sold by GEORGE GREENHILL, at their Hall, Ludgate-street, London'. 5,620 copies of the almanack were printed.

The new station at London Bridge is viewed from the forecourt. Passengers make their way to the general booking office at the centre of the building. Wealthy passengers wishing to take their carriages on the train head for and pass through the gate at the southern end. An elderly countryman, perhaps lost, consults a policeman.

In 1840 an Act was passed for the widening of the Greenwich Railway, allowing the construction of lines for the Brighton and Dover Companies. This necessitated the building of a new terminus. The architects appointed were Henry Roberts (1802–76) for the joint companies, and George Smith (1793–1869) for the Greenwich Railway. The building was completed in 1844. Its style was Italian Palazzo. An interesting feature was the observation campanile which commanded a view of the railway for several miles. The whole building stood on a massive substructure of piers and arches.

Copies seen: BM; GrPL; LMA; LMA-GL; RL; SC

1846

THE SOUTH END OF ST. JAMES'S STREET, THE NEW CLUB HOUSE, AND ST. JAMES'S PALACE. (ON A DRAWING-ROOM DAY)

Drawn by J. Marchant.

Engraved by H. Adlard.

215 × 406 mm

Steel engraving

In top margin: 'STATIONERS' [Company's arms] ALMANACK 1846'. In bottom margin, below the almanack text: 'Chiswick: Printed by C. WHITTINGHAM, for the COMPANY OF STATIONERS; and sold by GEORGE

GREENHILL, at their Hall, Ludgate-street, London'. 5,896 copies of the almanack were printed.

The club-house referred to is the Conservative Club, shown on the right. This Club was founded in 1840 for those who found it difficult to join the Carlton Club without a long wait. The new Palladian building was designed by Sydney Smirke (1797–1877) and George Basevi Junior (1794–1845), and built on the site of the Thatched Cottage Tavern at 74 St James's Street. It opened to members early in 1845. In the opinion of the *British Almanac* contributor, 1845, it was, 'after Royal Exchange, the most striking and richest piece of architecture that has for some time been executed in the metropolis'. At the end of the street is St James's Palace. The white building four doors down from the Conservative Club is the St James's Royal Hotel.

In 1950 the Conservative Club merged with the Bath Club, which continued to occupy the building until 1959, moved to Brook Street, and disbanded in 1981.

Queen Victoria's Drawing Room Days were, in effect, the equivalent of today's Buckingham Palace Garden Parties, but held indoors. Guests arrive (from left to right) in a coach, a town chariot, a nobleman's state coach, and a nobleman's state chariot.

Copies seen: BM; CUL; LMA-GL; ML; RL; SC; SMHSP; WesCA

*1846

THE BANK OF ENGLAND AND ROYAL EXCHANGE, LONDON.

202 × 416 mm

Steel engraving

There is related, unsigned pen and wash drawing in the London Metropolitan Archives (City KC 690). A related oil painting was auctioned at Christie's, 10

June 2003 (lot 78), together with a companion oil of the Mansion House, Poultry and Prince's Street (*[*c.*1861]).

On the left the Bank of England, in the centre the Royal Exchange and on the right the Globe Insurance Office. The third Royal Exchange, designed by Sir William Tite (1798–1873), was opened by Queen Victoria on 28 Oct. 1844. Within the pediment can now be seen Richard Westmacott's sculpture, with seventeen figures, the central figure being Commerce. Through the doorway one has a glimpse of the central quadrangle, open to the sky. Sir Francis Chantrey's statue of Wellington in front of the Royal Exchange had been installed on 18 June 1844. The staffage on the engraving includes several omnibuses, a hansom cab and in the centre what appears to be a laundry cart.

State 1
In top margin: 'STATIONER'S ALMANACK, 1846'. Beneath image: 'Engraved by T. A. Prior, from a Drawing by A.L. Thomas. Published by J. & W. Robins, 57 Tooley Street, London'. At bottom right of almanack text: 'LONDON: – Printed & Published by J. & W. ROBINS, 57, Tooley Street, Southwark'.
Copies seen: BM; LMA-GL; RL

State 2
Plate [16] in Anderson. Title and imprint removed. 'A. L. Thomas, pinx. T. A. Prior, sculp'.
Copies seen: GL

State 3
Modern impression.
Copies seen: LMA-GL

1847

WEST FRONT OF THE HORSE GUARDS.

Drawn by J. Marchant.
Engraved by H. Adlard.
212 × 402 mm
Steel engraving

The Palladian Horse Guards, headquarters of the General Staff, is viewed from St James's Park, which perhaps explains why women and children come to be mixed up in this essentially military scene. The Guards are perhaps rehearsing for the Trooping the Colour. Two children on the left, with their nanny and mother, ride in a phaeton-style goat cart.

Horse Guards was designed by William Kent (?1685–1748), and built 1751–3. (The Treasury building shown on the extreme right was also

designed by Kent.) In 1847 there were rumours that Sir Charles Barry had prepared plans for a complete *rifacimento* of the building.

State 1
In top margin: 'STATIONERS' [Company's arms] ALMANACK, 1847'. In bottom margin, below the almanack text: 'Chiswick: Printed by C. WHITTINGHAM, for the COMPANY OF STATIONERS; and sold by GEORGE GREENHILL, at their Hall, Ludgate-street, London'. 5,410 copies of the almanack were printed.
Copies seen: BM; LMA-GL; RL; SC; Well; WesCA

State 2
Lithographic reproduction. In top margin: 'STATIONERS' COMPANY'S [arms] ALMANAC FOR 1932'. In margin below almanack text: 'PUBLISHED BY THE WORSHIPFUL COMPANY OF STATIONERS, STATIONERS' HALL, E.C.4., AND TO BE OBTAINED FROM CHARLES LETTS & CO., SOUTHWARK BRIDGE BUILDINGS, LONDON S.E.1, OR ANY BOOKSELLER'. Priced at 2*s*. Text on it incorrectly states that the image had been originally used on the almanack for 1845.
Copies seen: CUL; LMA-GL

1848

THE NEW PUBLIC OFFICES AT WHITEHALL.

Drawn by J. Marchant.
Engraved by H. Adlard.
226 × 394 mm
Steel engraving

1846, see p. 44

1847, see p. 45

In top margin: 'STATIONERS' [Company's arms] ALMANACK 1848'. Immediately beneath the image identifications for the Privy Council, the Board of Trade, the Treasury and the Home Office. In bottom margin, below the almanack text: 'Chiswick: Printed by C. WHITTINGHAM, for the COMPANY OF STATIONERS; and sold by GEORGE GREENHILL, at their Hall, Ludgate-street, London'. 5,374 copies of the almanack were printed. The Company spent £3 9s. 3d. on advertising it. Marchant's related pencil drawing is the collection of the Museum of London.

The Public Offices (later the Treasury) as remodelled between 1844 and 1845 by Sir Charles Barry (1795–1860), to match his new Home Office, stretch from Downing Street on the left to York House on the right. The building was raised a storey and Sir John Soane's columns were reused (compare with *Stationers' Almanack*, 1827). The staffage includes an

omnibus and gig on the left, and at centre a troop of Guards, a town chariot and a state chariot.

Copies seen: BM; LMA; LMA-GL; ML; RL; SA; Well

*1848

THE NEW TREASURY OFFICES, WHITEHALL

C. Barry Esqre. R.A. Architect.

[Thomas Allom del.]

Engraved by T. A. Prior.

Published by J. & W. Robins, 57, Tooley Street, London.

200 × 410 mm

Steel engraving

In top margin: 'STATIONERS ALMANACK 1848'. At bottom right of almanack text: 'LONDON: –

Printed & Published by J. & W. ROBINS, 57, Tooley Street, Southwark'. Privy Council, Board of Trade, Treasury and Home Office keyed in bottom margin. A related drawing (pencil and sepia wash, heightened with white) was auctioned at Christie's South Kensington, 18 Nov. 1985 (lot 22). It was then listed in May 1986 in Christopher Wood Gallery catalogue. The print is listed as No. 1252 in *Index to British Military Costume Prints* (London: Army Museums Ogilby Trust, 1972).

See note for **1848**. This was one of the only years in which the official almanack and its rival chose the same subject. The view looks north down Whitehall to Trafalgar Square, with the new Treasury building, Dover House, formerly the Duke of York's, and Horse Guards on the left, and the garden of Montagu House and the Banqueting Hall on the right. In the distance is Trafalgar Square with the National Gallery and Nelson's Column. (The Column with its reliefs would not be completed until 1854; Landseer's lions were added in 1867.) The staffage includes a town chariot on the left, with a crossing sweeper nearby; and two Horse Guards in the centre, with more coming up at the rear.

Copies seen: BM; LMA; LMA-GL; RL; SMHSP; WesCA

1849

THE NEW EXTENDED FRONT OF BUCKINGHAM PALACE.

Drawn by J. Marchant.
Engraved by H. Adlard.
205 × 400 mm
Steel engraving

In top margin: 'STATIONERS' [Company's arms] ALMANACK, 1849'. In bottom margin, below almanack text: 'Chiswick: Printed by C. WHITTINGHAM, for the COMPANY OF STATIONERS; and sold by GEORGE GREENHILL,

at their Hall, Ludgate-street, London'. 5,383 copies of the almanack were printed. There is a related pencil drawing in the London Metropolitan Archives (ex-Guildhall Library, see below). Though the name of T. Hosmer Shepherd appears beneath the image in capitals, it is not in his style and must be by J. Marchant.

Following the death of George IV in 1830, the Government commissioned Edward Blore (1787–1879) to 'finish and ornament' Nash's design for a sum of £100,000. Blore's alterations included the new Park Front shown here (built 1846–7), which linked the two wings and closed off Nash's forecourt. Marble Arch was banished to Park Lane. (The *British Almanac* had suggested it become an entrance to the British Museum, with porter's lodges on either side.) In the foreground of Marchant's image, officers, splendidly attired, chat to admiring and unchaperoned ladies. Groups of visitors, some from the country, enjoy the military spectacle that is taking place in the palace grounds. Blore's park front would be replaced by Sir Aston Webb's in 1913.

Copies seen: BM; LMA-GL; RL; SC; Well; WesCA

1850

THE ZOOLOGICAL GARDENS IN THE REGENT'S PARK.

Drawn by J. Marchant.
Engraved by H. Adlard.
210 × 392 mm
Steel engraving

In top margin: 'STATIONERS' [Company's arms] ALMANACK, 1850'. In bottom margin, below almanack text: 'Chiswick: Printed by C. WHITTINGHAM, for the COMPANY OF STATIONERS; and sold by JOSEPH GREENHILL, at their Hall, Ludgate-street, London'. 5,390 copies of the almanack were printed.

The Regent's Park Zoo was laid out by Decimus Burton in 1827, and opened in 1828. Initially, only members of the Zoological Society and their friends were admitted, but in 1847, faced with financial problems, the Society was obliged to open it to the general public — admittance 1s. normally, 6d. on Mondays.

On the left in this view is the Carnivora Terrace, a superior menagerie, designed by Edmund Wallace Elmslie (fl. 1841–72) and erected in 1843. Its roof formed a terrace platform from which the Zoo and Regent's Park could be viewed. In the distance in the centre can be seen the encaged Polar Bear Pond. To right of centre the building with a clock tower is the Camel House designed by Burton. The elephant would either have been Jack, who died in 1847, or an anticipated replacement.

Copies seen: BM; LMA-GL; RL; SC; WesCA-M

*1850

WESTMINSTER, from Bishop's Walk, Lambeth.

[Thomas Allom del.?]

205 × 414 mm

Steel engraving

Principal buildings keyed below image. The steel plate probably survives: modern impressions have been made from it.

In the foreground on the right are the entrance to Lambeth Palace and St Mary's Lambeth. On the left is Lambeth Pier. A man is to be seen caulking

upturned boats on the shore nearby. On the River Thames itself are steamboats and Thames barges. Spectators on the Lambeth shore watch a boat race. Westminster Abbey and the new Houses of Parliament appear in the background, with stairs that were never built. It was at this point on the Lambeth shore that the Stationers moored their barge when paying their respects to the Archbishop of Canterbury on Lord Mayor's Day.

No artist's name appears on the print, but the style is very much that of Thomas Allom. Moreover, the detail of the Houses of Parliament closely relates to one in a pair of watercolour perspectives of Parliament by Thomas Allom which Sir Charles Barry presented to Tsar Nicholas I during his visit to London in 1842 and which is now in the Scientific Research Museum of the Russian Academy of Fine Arts. The Tsar's drawing made at an earlier date shows Parliament with Barry's rejected design for an extremely tall ventilation tower. A watercolour drawing of Lambeth Palace and St Mary's Lambeth, attributed perhaps wrongly to Allom, was auctioned at Christie's on 9 Nov. 1993 (lot 149).

State 1
In top margin: 'STATIONER'S ALMANACK, 1850'. Beneath image: 'T. A. PRIOR, SCULPT. Published by J. & W. Robins, 57, Tooley Street, London'. At bottom right of almanack text: 'LONDON: – Printed & Published by J. & W. ROBINS, 57, Tooley Street, Southwark'.

Copies seen: BM; LMA; LamPL; RL

State 2
Plate [15] in Anderson. Title and imprint removed. 'T. A. Prior, sculp'.

Copies seen: GL

State 3
Modern impression. T. A. Prior's details removed.

Copies seen: LMA-GL

1851

THE NEW COAL EXCHANGE, THAMES STREET, AT THE CEREMONY OF ITS OPENING IN 1849.

Drawn by J. Salman.

Engraved by H. Adlard.

210 × 400 mm

Steel engraving

In t. margin: 'STATIONERS' [Company arms] ALMANACK, 1851'. In b. margin, below almanack text: 'Chiswick: Printed by C. WHITTINGHAM, for the COMPANY OF STATIONERS; and sold by JOSEPH GREENHILL, at their Hall, Ludgate-street, London'. 5,150 copies of almanack were printed.

J. B. Bunning's Coal Exchange was erected at the corner of Lower Thames Street and St Mary at Hill between 1847 and 1849. The completed building was meant to be opened by Queen Victoria, but she being ill it was opened on 30 Oct. 1849 by Prince Albert. Before completion the *British Almanac* (1849) intemperately denounced it as 'anomalous and incoherent in every respect. Not only is it full of incongruities as a general composition but many of its features and details are not merely poor and bad but absolutely barbarous and indescribably grotesque ...'. After the royal opening (1850 *Almanac*) it moderated its language substantially: 'With some defects of taste it is a really handsome architectural mass'.

The engraving records the moment when Prince Albert, accompanied by the royal children, the Prince of Wales and the Princess Royal, was greeted by Alderman Sir James Duke, Lord Mayor. This ceremony took place in a grand pavilion that had been erected for the occasion, but in order to show the Exchange building to best advantage the artist has chosen to ignore its existence. A band of the Grenadier Guards plays on the left of the composition. There was much distress in 1963 when the Exchange was demolished so that Thames Street could be widened. The dragons, shown in this view, were removed and now mark the City boundary on the Victoria Embankment.

Copies seen: BM; LMA-GL; NMM; RL; SC

*1851

THE TOWER OF LONDON.

202 × 412 mm

Steel engraving

The steel plate probably survives: modern impressions have been made from it. Duncan's

drawing dated 1850 (pen and brown wash) is in the Museum of London (A 6988 (63B)).

At the back of the Tower of London, to the left of the White Tower, is to be seen a new castellated building. This is the Waterloo Barracks, built in 1845, and erected on the site of the Grand Storehouse, burnt down in 1841. The buoy in the river at bottom rignt is marked: 'E. Duncan 1850'.

State 1
In top margin: 'STATIONER'S ALMANACK, 1851'. Beneath image: 'Engraved by T. A. Prior, from a Drawing by E. Duncan. Published by J. & W. Robins, 57, Tooley Street, London'. At bottom right of almanack text: 'LONDON: – Printed & Published by J. & W. ROBINS, 57, Tooley Street, Southwark'.
Copies seen: BM; LMA; LMA-GL; RL

State 2
Plate [14] in Anderson. Title and imprint erased. 'E. Duncan, pinx. T. A. Prior, sculp'.
Copies seen: GL

State 3
Modern impression.
Copies seen: P

1852

THE SOUTH FRONT OF THE BRITISH MUSEUM.

Sir R. Smirke, R.A. Archt.

Drawn by F. Mackenzie.

Engraved by H. Adlard.

210 × 392 mm

Steel engraving

In top margin: 'STATIONERS' [Company's arms] ALMANACK 1852'. In bottom margin, below almanack text: 'Chiswick: Printed by C. WHITTINGHAM, for the COMPANY OF STATIONERS; and sold by JOSEPH GREENHILL, at their Hall, Ludgate-street, London'. 7,622 copies of the almanack were printed. The British Museum has a copy of Sir Robert Smirke's official lithograph of 1844, drawn by Frederick Mackenzie, printed by F. C. Cheffins (1901-5-8-1 British Imperial Period V). A flap has been attached to the courtyard area of this print, and upon it Mackenzie has drawn appropriate staffage, in watercolour touched with white and graphite. He has also drawn figures mounting the BM steps on the lithograph itself. This composite image has then been re-engraved to become this *Stationers' Almanack*.

Being a copy of Robert Smirke's perspective, this image shows the front of the building as proposed, not precisely as built. It has statues on the roofline, and sculptures of the 'Wrestlers' and the 'Laocoon' on either side of the steps. The Museum's southern colonnade was completed in 1847. The building excited little interest, its style by this time being considered out of date.

Copies seen: BM; CamPL; CUL; LMA; LMA-GL; RL; SC

*1852

THE GREAT EXHIBITION, 1851. TRANSEPT LOOKING NORTH.

Drawn on the Spot & Engraved by T. A. Prior.
Published by J. & W. Robins, 57, Tooley Street, London.
1210 × 412 mm
Steel engraving

The steel plate probably survives: modern impressions have been made from it.

The Great Exhibition was opened by Queen Victoria on 1 May 1851. In the mid-distance the Queen, Prince Albert, and two of their children (Vicky and Bertie?), together with their retinue, view the Exhibition. (The Queen paid the Exhibition frequent visits —twelve times just in May.) In the centre is to be seen F. & C. Osler's Crystal Fountain, the central feature of the Crystal Palace. Twenty-seven feet high, it was made from four tons of pure crystal glass. Beyond is a living elm tree which the Great Exhibition Building Committee had stipulated should not be cut down, making it necessary for Joseph Paxton to design his glass exhibition hall around it. On the left is the India section, extensive and greatly admired. The statuary, on the other hand, heroic, moralizing and sentimental, attracted criticism.

State 1
In top margin: 'STATIONER'S ALMANACK, 1852'. Beneath image: 'Drawn on the Spot & Engraved by T. A. Prior. Published by J. & W. Robins, 57, Tooley Street, London'. At bottom right of almanack text: 'LONDON:– Printed & Published by J. & W. ROBINS, 57, Tooley Street, Southwark'.
Copies seen: RL

State 2
Modern impression. Information erased from top margin.
Copies seen: LMA-GL

1853

THE ARMY AND NAVY CLUB HOUSE, PALL MALL.

Drawn by J. Marchant.
Engraved by H. Adlard.
205 × 392 mm
Steel engraving

In top margin: 'STATIONERS' [Company's arms] ALMANACK 1853'. In bottom margin, below almanack text: 'Printed by C. WHITTINGHAM, Tooks Court, Chancery Lane, for the COMPANY OF STATIONERS, and sold by JOSEPH GREENHILL, at their Hall, Ludgate-street, London'. There is a related pencil drawing in the London Metropolitan Archives (Westminster DD 7545). Though the name of T. Hosmer Shepherd appears beneath it in capitals, it is not in his style and must be by J. Marchant. The London Metropolitan Archives also have a related drawing in sepia pen and wash with body colour (ex-Guildhall Library — Pr. W2/PAL). 5,164 copies of the almanack were printed.

The Army & Navy Club, with its imposing Venetian exterior, was erected on the north side of Pall Mall, on the corner of George Street, between 1848 and 1851. (Note: privileged men enter and exit the Club: their ladies remain dutifully outside.) The club house had been designed by Charles Octavius Parnell (1807–65) and Alfred Smith. The almanack's image may be derived from the architects' perspective (lithographed by G. Hawkins and reproduced in *Getting London in Perspective* (London: Barbican Art Gallery, 1984), p. 65. The *British Almanac* announced: 'The Army and Navy Club at length exposes its finished exterior, and with its huge toppling load strikes terror and amazement into ... passengers in Pall Mall'. The Army and Navy Club House was demolished in 1963.

Advancing down Pall Mall on the left is a state chariot.

Copies seen: BM; LMA; LMA-GL; ML; RL; SC

*1853

THE SUSPENSION BRIDGE AT CHELSEA, NOW IN COURSE OF CONSTRUCTION FOR THE COMMISSIONERS OF HER MAJESTY'S WORKS, AND ROYAL MILITARY HOSPITAL.

[Thomas Allom del.]

200 × 412 mm

Steel engraving

What may have been Thomas Allom's related perspective was exhibited at the Royal Academy in 1851 (315). A related Allom drawing (pencil, pen, sepia ink and wash, heightened with white) was auctioned at the Allom sale at Christie's South Kensington, 18 Nov. 1985 (lot 23). For the print, see No. 301 in E. Longford, *Images of Chelsea* (Richmond-upon-Thames: St Helena Press, 1980).

Pimlico, developed by Thomas Cubitt (1788–1855), lacked a public open space. On Cubitt's urging the Government purchased Battersea

Fields and transformed them into Battersea Park. The Park was opened in 1854. Chelsea Suspension Bridge, linking Pimlico to Battersea, was designed by Thomas Page (1803–77), who also designed Westminster Bridge and the Albert

Embankment. Building work had commenced in 1852; it would not be completed until 1858. The iron work would be painted tea-green picked out with gold. With the exception of the toll houses at either end it would be generally admired. Within two years of the opening, however, the view of the bridge from the east would be obscured by the Victoria Railway Bridge carrying the London, Chatham & Dover Railway to Victoria Station. Page's Chelsea Suspension Bridge would be replaced by Rendel, Palmer & Tritton's Chelsea Bridge in 1937.

In the background behind the Chelsea Bridge can be seen the Royal Hospital Chelsea, and to the right of it St Gabriel's, Warwick Square. On the river the Oxford and Cambridge boat race appears to be in progress, the oarsmen cheered on by spectators who stand on the Battersea bank and on the roadway and piers of the new bridge. The Stationers' State Barge proceeds upstream, its destination most probably Richmond. A Thames sailing barge lowers its sail to pass beneath the bridge.

State 1
In top margin: 'STATIONER'S ALMANACK, 1853'. Beneath image: 'THOS. PAGE, ENGINEER. T. A. PRIOR, ENGRAVER. Published Nov. 18, 1852, by J. & W. Robins, 57 Tooley Street, London'. At bottom right of almanack text: 'LONDON: – Printed & Published by J. & W. ROBINS, 57, Tooley Street, Southwark'.

Copies seen: BM; LMA-GL; NMM; RL; WesCA

State 2
Title, engraver, engineer and imprint erased from margin beneath image. 'T. A. Prior, sculp'. Plate [18] in Anderson.

Copies seen: GL; LMA

1854

THE ROYAL BOTANICAL GARDENS AT KEW.

Drawn by W. Lacey.

Engraved by H. Adlard.

206 × 396 mm

Steel engraving

In top margin: 'STATIONERS' [Company arms] ALMANACK 1854'. In bottom margin, below almanack text: 'Printed by C. WHITTINGHAM, Tooks Court, Chancery Lane, for the COMPANY OF STATIONERS; and sold by JOSEPH GREENHILL, at their Hall, Ludgate-street, London'. 5,150 copies of the almanack were printed. The Company spent £4 0s. 6d. on advertising it. The advertisement is to be seen in *The Times*, 26 Dec. 1853.

Kew Gardens date from the eighteenth century and possibly earlier. The buildings in this image, however, were recent. The principal building is the Palm House, erected 1844–48, and in front of it the tropical water-lily house, erected 1852. The Palm House was designed by Decimus Burton (1800–81), and the engineer was Richard Turner (c.1798–1846). Peeping over the trees is the campanile, designed by Burton, and erected in 1847. It served as the chimney for the furnaces underneath the Palm House.

Copies seen: BM; LMA-GL; RL; SC

1855

THE NEW BRIDGE AND PALACE AT WESTMINSTER.

SIR CHARLES BARRY, ARCHT.

Drawn by P. Phillips.

Engraved by H. Adlard.

210 × 420 mm

Steel engraving

Heading in top margin: 'STATIONERS' [Company arms] ALMANACK 1855'. For his 'drawing & sketch' for the 1855 *Stationers' Almanack*, the

Company paid Phillips £31 10s. 0d. 6,447 copies of the almanack were printed. The Company spent £5 17s. 0d. on advertising it.

The Houses of Parliament are shown from the river as if completed. Victoria Tower and the Central Tower are shown more or less as constructed. The unfinished Clock Tower, however, has been equipped with a tall, ornate and slender spire, increasing its height considerably. In the background on the right, Westminster Abbey looms over other buildings.

The new Westminster Bridge was designed by Thomas Page (1803–77), Sir Charles Barry (1795–1860) acting as architectural consultant. The old bridge had to serve as a temporary bridge whilst the construction was in progress. Work began in May 1854 but was suspended on 20 March 1856 when the contractors failed. In 1858 after much debate it was accepted that too much work had already been done to seek an alternative site, and work began again. The bridge was completed in 1862. It consists of seven low segmented arches of wrought and cast iron borne on solid granite piers. The approaches having been raised, it was of much lower gradient than the old bridge. Its width for London bridges at that time was unparalleled — 85 feet.

State 1:
Title, etc. as above. Spire of Clock Tower not as built. No Westminster Pier.

Copies seen: BM; LMA-GL (proof); RL

State 2:
Title: 'THE HOUSES OF PARLIAMENT AND WESTMINSTER ABBEY'. Architect, artist, and engraver's names removed. Heading: 'STATIONERS' COMPANY'S [Company's arms] ALMANAC FOR 1899'. In bottom margin, below the almanack text: 'Printed and Published for the Stationers' Company, London, by CHARLES LETTS & CO., 3, Royal Exchange, E.C'. Image has been changed to show the Palace of Westminster's Clock Tower as actually built. Westminster Pier has been added, and also new buildings on the Victoria

Embankment. These include Norman Shaw's New Scotland Yard, built 1888–90 (see p. 67).

Copies seen: LMA-GL

*[c.1861]

CITY OF LONDON. MANSION HOUSE, POULTRY AND PRINCES STREET.

Drawn by G. Chambers [Junior].

Engraved by T. A. Prior.

Published by John Robins, 57, Tooley Street, Southwark.

206 × 408 mm

Steel engraving

A related oil painting was auctioned at Christie's, 10 June 2003 (lot 78), together with an oil painting related to the headpiece for the *Stationers' Almanack* *1846. The steel plate for the engraving probably survives: modern impressions have been made from it. The original drawing in pencil with grey wash and bodycolour is in the collection of the Museum of London. It is reproduced in Alan Russett, *George Chambers, 1803–1840: His Life and Work* (Woodbridge: Antique Collectors' Club, 1996), p. 195.

An autumn or winter scene: one woman on the right wears a muff. Beyond Poultry in Cheapside is to be seen St Mary-le-Bow; within Poultry itself is the Wren church of St Mildred Poultry, demolished in 1872. The corner of the Bank of England appears on the extreme right. The Bank Beadle directs some ladies who are clearly lost. Other detail includes eight knifeboard omnibuses, a hansom cab, what appear to be the Bank Volunteers (rather than the Bank Picket), and various pedestrians.

State 1
As above.

Copies seen: LMA-GL

State 2
No imprint.

Copies seen: LMA

*1862

WINDSOR CASTLE, FROM CLEWER MEADOWS.

202 × 402 mm

Steel engraving

The steel plate probably survives: modern impressions have been made from it.

State 1
In top margin: 'STATIONER'S ALMANACK 1862'. In bottom margin: 'Drawn by E. Duncan. Engraved by T. A. Prior. London. Published by J. Robins, Tooley Street'. At bottom right of almanack text: 'London. – Printed & Published by JOHN ROBINS, 57, Tooley Street, Southwark'.

Copies seen: RL

State 2
'E. Duncan, pinx. T. A. Prior, sculp'. No heading, title, or imprint. Plate [1] in Anderson.

Copies seen: GL; RL

State 3
Modern impression.

Copies seen: P

1866

THE ELEANOR CROSS AND CHARING CROSS HOTEL.

Drawn by John O'Connor.

Engraved by H. Adlard.

212 × 400 mm

Steel engraving

In top margin: 'STATIONERS COMPANY'S [arms] ALMANACK FOR 1866'. In margin below almanack text: 'Printed by WHITTINGHAM AND WILKINS, Tooks Court, Chancery Lane, for the Company of Stationers, and sold by JOSEPH GREENHILL, at their Hall, Ludgate-street, London'.

The Company paid O'Connor £21 0s. 0d. for undertaking the drawing. They had 6,702 copies printed, and spent £2 12s. 6d. on advertising it.

*[*c.1861*]**, see p. 55

The Charing Cross Hotel, set back from the Strand and extending down Villiers Street, was designed by E. M. Barry (1830–80) and built 1863–4. Large and imposing hotels were becoming a feature of London just then: the Grosvenor Hotel at Victoria and the Langham Hotel at the north end of Upper Regent Street had recently been completed. The Charing Cross Hotel would have railway booking offices at street level, and luxury rooms including an opulent dining room and 250 bedrooms above. In 1864–5 Barry erected in the forecourt Thomas Earp's free reproduction of the Eleanor Cross. The heap of masonry in the foreground hints at its recent erection. The original cross, which stood close by and gave the location its name, was demolished in 1647. Passengers are delivered by victoria, hansom cab and brougham to the pavement adjacent to the new station's ticket office, where railway porters assist them with their trunks. On the left on the north side of the Strand is to be seen Sir Robert Smirke's façade for the 'Pepper-pot Building', which today houses Coutts' Bank. On its roof you can see a glass cone. This is probably the most famous glasshouse of all the early London photographic studios, opened by the pioneer photographer, Antoine Claudet, in June 1841. By the early 1860s the studio was in the hands of a Congregational minister named Schnadhorst, who changed his name to Hughes. (Information on the studio kindly supplied by David Webb.)

Copies seen: LMA-GL (proof); RL; WesAC

*1866

THAMES EMBANKMENT.

205 × 422 mm

Steel engraving

Temple Gardens and Pier, and new Blackfriars Bridge keyed in margin beneath image. The steel plate probably survives: modern impressions have been made from it.

The Victoria Embankment was the most ambitious of the Metropolitan Board of Works' improvements. It tidied up the north bank of the Thames, sweeping away the clutter of wharves, and provided the capital with a new highway, beneath which was the new main sewer and also the new District underground railway. The image shows the scheme, designed by Sir Joseph Bazalgette (1819–1891), as intended, not as realized. The equestrian statues shown at the City end of Blackfriars Bridge were never built, and Temple steamboat pier would be far less imposing. An imaginary occasion of some importance is depicted: pier, boats, bridge, and Embankment are lined with crowds. The new Blackfriars Bridge, designed by Joseph Cubitt (1811–72), would be opened by Queen Victoria on 6 Nov. 1869. The Embankment would be opened by the Prince of Wales on 13 July 1870.

State 1
In top margin: 'STATIONERS' ALMANACK 1866'. Beneath the image: 'Drawn by G. H. Andrews. Engraved by T. A. Prior. London, Published Novr. 1865 by Brook & Roberts, late J. Robins, 57, Tooley Street, S.E'. At bottom right of almanack text: 'London: Printed & Published by BROOK & ROBERTS (late J. ROBINS), Tooley Street, S.E'.
Copies seen: LMA-GL; RL

State 2
Text in bottom margin for State 1 erased, and 'G. H. Andrews, pinx. T. A. Prior, sculp' introduced. Plate [13] in Anderson.
Copies seen: GL; LMA-GL

State 3
Modern impression
Copies seen: LMA-GL

1867

THE NEW GOVERNMENT OFFICES FROM ST. JAMES'S PARK.

Drawn by John O'Connor.
Engraved by Henry Adlard.

212 × 393 mm

Steel engraving

In top margin: 'STATIONERS' COMPANY'S [arms] ALMANACK FOR 1867'. In bottom margin, below the almanack text: 'Printed by WHITTINGHAM AND WILKINS, Tooks Court, Chancery Lane, for the COMPANY OF STATIONERS; and sold by JOSEPH GREENHILL, at their Hall, Ludgate-street, London'. The Company paid O'Connor £21 0s. 0d. for undertaking the drawing. They had 6,352 copies of the almanack printed, and spent £2 15s. 6d. on advertising it. The advertisement appeared in *The Times*, 14 Dec. 1866.

George Gilbert Scott's Palladian-style Government Offices, housing the Home Office, the Colonial Office, the India Office and Foreign Office, were constructed between 1868 and 1873. This view of the building as seen from St James's Park is based on Scott's drawings of May 1861, signed by the Chancellor of the Exchequer. On the far left in this image is Horse Guards where a parade is in progress. Where the new building is concerned the Foreign Office is on the left, and the India Office in the centre and on the right. The skyline sculpture shown on the building was never executed. (For companion print for Parliament Street front of the building, see **1875**.)

Copies seen: CUL; LMA; LMA-GL; RL; SC

1868

CANNON STREET STATION AND BRIDGE FROM THE THAMES.

Drawn by John O'Connor.

Engraved by H. Adlard.

210 × 386 mm

Steel engraving

In top margin: 'STATIONERS' COMPANY'S [arms] ALMANACK FOR 1868'. In bottom margin, below the almanack text: 'Printed for WHITTINGHAM AND WILKINS, Tooks Court,

Chancery Lane, for the COMPANY OF STATIONERS; and sold by JOSEPH GREENHILL, at their Hall, Ludgate-street, London'. The Company paid O'Connor £21 0s. 0d. for undertaking the drawing. They had 6,618 copies printed, and spent £3 14s. 6d. on advertising it.

The South Eastern Railway's extension to the City was constructed between 1863 and 1866. The bridge for it very nearly matched that built for the extension to Charing Cross further up river, and the terminus hotel in Cannon Street also bore a close resemblance to the hotel at Charing Cross Station. This was hardly surprising since both bridges were designed by Sir John Hawkshaw (1811–91), and both hotels by E. M. Barry (1830–80). The Cannon Street Railway Bridge came in for plenty of criticism. The weight of the bridge was borne by sixteen iron piers, ranged behind each other in fours so as to offer minimum resistance to the current. It carried a rather ungainly semaphore signal box. No facilities were offered for pedestrians to ease the pressure on nearby London Bridge. James Thorne in the *British Almanac* for 1867 considered both bridge and station a 'grievous drawback' to the picturesqueness of the Thames. 'The fine view from London Bridge of St Paul's is utterly destroyed by the huge and irredeemably hideous roof of the railway terminus.'

Copies seen: LMA-GL; RL; SC

*1868

THE THAMES AT RICHMOND.

Drawn by G. H. Andrews.

Engraved by T. A. Prior.

210 × 400 mm

Steel engraving

The steel plate probably survives: modern impressions have been made from it. There is a

*1868

related watercolour drawing, signed G. H. Andrews, at the London Metropolitan Archives (ex-Guildhall Library). The print is listed as no. 520 in B. Gascoigne, *Images of Richmond* (Richmond-upon-Thames: St Helena Press, 1978).

Each Master of the Stationers' Company during his term of office was entitled to the single use of the Company's barge for an excursion to Richmond. Lord Mayors were in the habit of taking the City barge to Richmond, too. The ladies were provided with coaches to take them up the hill for dinner at the Star and Garter, rebuilt in the style of a French château by E. M. Barry in 1868 (see Michael Osborne, *The State Barges of the Stationers' Company* (London: Company of Stationers, 1972)). The barge shown in this headpiece flying the white ensign would seem to be the last City Barge – the *Maria Wood*.

State 1
In top margin: 'STATIONERS' ALMANACK 1868'. Beneath image: 'London, Published Novr. 1867 by Brook & Roberts, late J. Robins, 57, Tooley Street, S.E'. At bottom right of almanack text: 'London: Printed & Published by BROOK & ROBERTS (late J. ROBINS), Tooley Street, S.E'.
Copies seen: LMA-GL; RL

State 2
Modern impression.
Copies seen: LMA-GL

*[1870?]
ALBERT MEMORIAL, HYDE PARK.

Drawn by G. H. Andrews.
Engraved by T. A. Prior.
215 × 393 mm
Steel engraving

The steel plate probably survives: modern impressions have been made from it.

Prince Albert died on 14 Dec. 1861. A month later the Lord Mayor of London convened a meeting at the Mansion House at which it was resolved that a monument should be erected to the memory of 'our blameless Prince'. Funds were to be raised by public subscription and vote of Parliament, and Hyde Park was chosen as the site. Seven architects were invited to submit designs. It was those of Sir George Gilbert Scott (1811–78), resembling a Gothic reliquary, that were adopted. By July 1872 the

Memorial was complete except for the statue of Albert. This was put in place in 1876.

The Albert Memorial part of this image is derived from Scott's watercolour perspective, now in the V&A's collection (reproduced in *Getting London in Perspective* (London: Barbican Art Gallery, 1984), p. 33. Scott made this drawing before adding an extra storey to the spire. There are also small details on the canopy of this early design that differ from those on the finished monument.

In the background and to the right of the Memorial is the Royal Albert Hall of Arts and Sciences, declared open by the Prince of Wales in 1870. The staffage includes a postilion-driven barouche, a man riding a 'bone-shaker' velocipede (its pedals attached to the front wheel) and a brougham. (The 'bone-shaker' was a five-minute wonder. Introduced in 1869, it is rarely seen on a print of any other date.)

State 1
Imprint: 'London, Published Novr. 1869, by Brook & Roberts, Tooley Street, S.E'.

Copies seen: ML

State 2
Modern impression. No heading.

Copies seen: LMA-GL

1873

THAMES EMBANKMENT FROM SOMERSET HOUSE.

Drawn by John O'Connor.

Engraved by H. Adlard.

202 × 375 mm

Signed on parapet: 'JOC 72'. The Museum of London has John O'Connor's oil version of the image. See Celina Fox, 'John O'Connor's Embankment', *National Art-Collections Fund Review* (1986); and Mireille Galinou and John Hayes, *London in Paint* (London: Museum of London, 1996), pp. 220–3. Galinou and Hayes provide a key to the image.

A handbill listing the almanacks published by the Stationers' Company announces:
Will be published on Thursday the 21st of November next ... Stationers' Company's sheet almanac 2.s. on super royal paper, is equally adapted for the Counting-house and the Library, containing lists of the chief Officers of State, Judges, Public Officers, London Bankers and Insurance Offices, with very copious Postal Information, is embellished with a VIEW OF THE THAMES EMBANKMENT FROM WATERLOO BRIDGE, LOOKING EAST,

of which Proof Impressions on thick paper may be had at 3s. each ...Proof Impressions of the Embellishment of the Stationers' Company's Sheet Almanac are taken off on plate paper, and sold at 3s. each'.

In the manner of Canaletto, Antonio Joli and Paul Sandby, O'Connor produced a pair of Thames views, looking towards the City, and looking towards Westminster (see **1876** for companion view). The view is from the river terrace of Somerset House, now cut off from the Thames by the Victoria Embankment. Beyond Somerset House can be identified the spire of St Bride's, Middle Temple Hall, St Paul's, the gas holders of the City Gas Company (demolished 1873) and Cannon Street Station. On the river side of the Embankment is the Temple Steamboat Pier, the new Blackfriars Bridge, and immediately behind it Blackfriars Railway Bridge, used by the London, Chatham & Dover Railway. The trees at this date are newly planted saplings. A column of soldiers march in the direction of the City.

O'Connor exhibited his related oil painting at the Royal Academy in 1874 (no. 588). The *Illustrated London News* described it as 'a capital picture of London's latest improvement' (quoted by Fox). Galinou and Hayes suggest the engraving and the drawing for it were made before the oil version was painted. In the painting the man on the terrace admiring the view is replaced by a nursemaid with two children in her charge. She wears a crinoline dress without the frame, perhaps remodelled and passed down by her employer.

State 1
Steel engraving. In top margin: 'STATIONERS' COMPANY'S [arms] ALMANAC FOR 1873'. In bottom margin, below almanack text: 'Printed by HARRISON AND SONS, Printers in Ordinary to Her Majesty, St. Martin's Lane, for the COMPANY OF STATIONERS; and sold by JOSEPH GREENHILL, at their Hall, Ludgate Hill, London. Priced at Two shillings'

Copies seen: LMA; LMA-GL; SC

State 2
Steel engraving. Title: 'THAMES EMBANKMENT — THIRTY YEARS AGO'. In top margin: 'THE IMPERIAL. STATIONERS' COMPANY'S [arms] ALMANAC FOR 1905 THE IMPERIAL'. In bottom margin, below the almanack text: 'Printed and Published for the Stationers' Company, London, by CHARLES LETTS & CO., 3, Royal Exchange, E.C'.

Copies seen: LMA-GL; YCBA

1873 steel engraving.

State 3
Lithographic reproduction. In top margin:
'STATIONERS' COMPANY'S [arms] ALMANAC
FOR 1929'. In margin below almanack text:
'PUBLISHED BY THE WORSHIPFUL COMPANY
OF STATIONERS, STATIONERS' HALL, E.C.4.,
AND TO BE OBTAINED FROM MESSRS.
THOMAS DE LA RUE & COMPANY, LIMITED,
OR ANY BOOKSELLER. REGISTERED AT
STATIONERS' HALL'.
Copies seen: CUL; LMA-GL

1875

NEW GOVERNMENT BUILDINGS, PARLIAMENT STREET.

Drawn by John O'Connor.
Engraved by H. Adlard.
202 × 368 mm
Steel engraving

In top margin: 'STATIONERS' COMPANY'S [arms]
ALMANAC FOR 1875'. In bottom margin, below
the almanack text: 'Printed by HARRISON AND
SONS, Printer in Ordinary to Her Majesty, St.
Martin's Lane for the COMPANY OF
STATIONERS; and sold by JOSEPH GREENHILL,
at their Hall, Ludgate Hill, London. Price Two
Shillings'.

Sir George Gilbert Scott's Government Offices
were completed in 1873. Most of the sculpture
shown on the skyline never materialized. It
seems likely then that this view was copied from
one of the architect's perspectives.

On the left is the garden of Montagu House,
and looming over the buildings on that side of
Parliament Street are the Clock Tower and
Victoria Tower of the Houses of Parliament. On
the right of the street, the building nearest to us is
the Council Office, formerly called the Treasury.
In the distance, though largely obscured, is the
Henry VII Chapel of Westminster Abbey. For
companion print showing the St James's Park
front of the Government Offices, see **1867**.
Copies seen: LMA; LMA-GL; SC

Oil painting related to **1873** steel engraving.

1876

WESTMINSTER EMBANKMENT AND FLOATING BATH.

Drawn by John O'Connor.
Engraved by Henry Adlard.
202 × 368 mm
Steel engraving

In top margin: 'STATIONERS' COMPANY'S [arms] ALMANAC FOR 1876'. In bottom margin, below the almanack text: 'Printed by HARRISON AND SONS, Printers in Ordinary to Her Majesty, St. Martin's Lane for the COMPANY OF STATIONERS; and sold by JOSEPH GREENHILL, at their Hall, Ludgate Hill, London. Price Two Shillings'.

The view of the Victoria Embankment looking south towards Westminster Bridge, the Houses of Parliament, and Westminster Abbey is taken from Hungerford Bridge. The Embankment, lined with newly planted saplings, extends to Westminster Bridge Steamboat Pier. In the river on the left a tug with lighters makes its way downstream. Moored on the right is the floating swimming bath, enclosed in glass with flanking domes. This vessel was opened in July 1875. By Christmas that year it had been made into a glaciarium (ice-rink) with Robert C. Austin, 'champion skater of America', acting as 'Skating Manager and Instructor'. The vessel would be removed from its mooring when the Hungerford Bridge was widened in 1886.

See **1873** for companion view. O'Connor exhibited 'Westminster from Charing Cross — Evening' (a related painting?) at the R.A. in 1876 (no. 549).

Copies seen: BM; CUL; LMA-GL; SC

1877

WINDSOR CASTLE FROM THE GREAT WESTERN RAILWAY.

Drawn by John O'Connor.

Engraved by B. Lasbury.

202 × 375 mm

Steel engraving

In t. margin: 'STATIONERS' COMPANY'S [arms] ALMANAC FOR 1877'. In b. margin, below almanack text: 'Printed by HARRISON AND SONS, Printers in Ordinary to Her Majesty, St. Martin's Lane, for the COMPANY OF STATIONERS; and sold by JOSEPH GREENHILL, at their Hall, Ludgate Hill, London. Price Two Shillings'.

Copies seen: LMA-GL; SC

1880

THE NEW LAW COURTS.

Drawn by John O'Connor.

Engraved by John Saddler.

202 × 368 mm

Steel engraving

An advertisement appeared in *The Times*, 22 Nov. 1879.

The foundations for the new Law Courts in the Strand designed by G. E. Street (1824–81), were

laid in 1871–2. Construction work began in 1874. Street died of a stroke and overwork in 1881, and the building was completed by his son, A. E. Street (1855–1938), and Sir Arthur Blomfield (1829–99). The gallery of the tower of the Law Courts as shown in this image differs slightly from the tower as built. Queen Victoria would formally open the building on 4 Dec. 1882.

In the distance is Fleet Street with the tower of St Dunstan-in-the-West.

State 1

In top margin: 'STATIONERS COMPANY'S [arms] ALMANAC FOR 1880'. In bottom margin, below the almanack text: 'Printed by HARRISON AND SONS, Printers in Ordinary to Her Majesty, St. Martin's Lane, for the COMPANY OF STATIONERS; and sold by JOSEPH GREENHILL, at their Hall, Ludgate Hill, London. Price Two Shillings'.

Copies seen: LMA-GL; SC

State 2

Title: 'THE LAW COURTS'. In top margin: 'THE IMPERIAL. STATIONERS' COMPANY'S [arms] ALMANAC FOR 1904. THE IMPERIAL'. In bottom margin, below the almanack text: 'Printed and Published for the Stationers' Company, London, by CHARLES LETTS & CO., 3, Royal Exchange'. Artist's and engraver's names erased.

Copies seen: LMA-GL

1884

ST. PAUL'S CATHEDRAL AND THE CITY OF LONDON SCHOOL.

Drawn by John O'Connor A.R.H.A.

Engraved by John Saddler.

196 × 382 mm

Steel engraving

The City of London School, formerly in Milk Street off Cheapside, moved to new premises designed by Messrs Davis and Emanuel on the

Victoria Embankment in 1883. The site had most recently been occupied by the gas holders of the City Gas Company (see **1873**). Next to it, on the corner of the Embankment and New Bridge Street, is De Keyser's Royal Hotel. Two large sculptural groups can be seen flanking the City end of Blackfriars Bridge. In the event neither was put there, and it was a seated statue of Queen Victoria (who had opened the Bridge in 1869) which would be installed at this point in 1896. On the far side of Blackfriars Bridge can be seen the London, Chatham & Dover Railway's Blackfriars Railway Bridge, and the piers of a second railway bridge, the St Paul's Bridge, which at this date was under construction.

State 1

In top margin: 'STATIONERS' COMPANY'S [arms] ALMANAC FOR 1884'. In bottom margin, below the almanack text: 'Printed by HARRISON AND SONS, Printer in Ordinary to Her Majesty, St. Martin's Lane, for the STATIONER'S COMPANY, Stationer's Hall, Ludgate Hill, London. Price Two Shillings'.

Copies seen: LMA-GL; SC; Well

State 2

Lithographic reproduction. In top margin: 'STATIONERS' COMPANY'S [arms] ALMANACK FOR 1930'. In margin below almanack text: 'PUBLISHED BY THE WORSHIPFUL COMPANY OF STATIONERS, STATIONERS' HALL, E.C.4., AND TO BE OBTAINED FROM CHARLES LETTS & CO., SOUTHWARK BRIDGE BUILDINGS, LONDON S.E.1, OR ANY BOOKSELLER'. Priced at 2*s*.

Copies seen: CUL; LMA-GL

*[1886]

[HARROW ON THE HILL]

A. Duncan [del]

J. Godfrey [sculp]

London, Published July 15th 1885, by Roberts & Leete, 57 & 58 Tooley St.

202 × 393 mm

Steel engraving

Within the image at bottom left: 'A. Duncan'. See A. W. Ball, *Painting, Prints, and Drawings of Harrow* (London: Borough of Harrow, 1978), pp. 32–3.

The scene is of Harrow on the Hill, dominated by St Mary's Church and the buildings of Harrow School. A handbill, dated 1 Oct. 1885, was issued by J. C. Wilbee of the Harrow School Bookshop, which announced that the engraving

had just been finished. India proofs were already in the possession of the Very Revd Dr Butler, headmaster, and several of the Harrow masters and residents. '... I trust that you will avail yourself of one of the necessarily limited FIRST IMPRESSIONS of this LOW-PRICED yet GENUINE WORK OF ART.' The india proof would cost 7*s*. 6*d*., and frame for it a further 7*s*. 6*d*., and packing for rail or carrier 1*s*. The handbill carries a miniature version of the image, and identifies the scene as being the town of Harrow from the north-east (Kenton Lane).

Copies seen: LMA-GL; HarPL. LMA-GL has no sign of imprint.

1888

PUTNEY BRIDGE.

Drawn by John O'Connor R.I.

Engraved by John Saddler.

192 × 402 mm

Steel engraving

In top margin: 'STATIONERS' COMPANY'S [arms]

ALMANAC FOR 1888'. In bottom margin, below the almanack text: 'Printed by HARRISON AND SONS, Printers in Ordinary to Her Majesty, St. Martin's Lane, for the STATIONERS COMPANY, Stationers' Hall, Ludgate Hill, London. Price Two Shillings'.

Scene looking up-river with St Mary's Church on the left. Putney Pier can be seen through the arches of the bridge. The bridge, designed by Sir Joseph Bazalgette (1819–91), was completed in 1886. It replaced the wooden bridge built in 1729 by Thomas Phillips. The rowing boat with four oarsmen and a cox is evidence of the proximity of rowing clubs. Putney Bridge has been the starting point of the Oxford and Cambridge boat race since 1845.

Copies seen: LMA-GL; SC; WanPL

1890

THE TOWER OF LONDON.

Drawn by Louis Godfrey.

Engraved by Louis Godfrey.

196 × 386 mm

Steel engraving

Within image at bottom left: 'Louis. Godfrey'.

Crudely drawn view of the Tower by an artist with little understanding of perspective. The building on the extreme right must be a warehouse of St Katharine's Dock, but there is no evidence of Tower Bridge which by this date was under construction.

State 1
In top margin: 'STATIONERS' COMPANY'S [arms] ALMANAC FOR 1890'. Advertised in *British Almanac* for 1890.

Copies seen: LMA-GL; SC

State 2
Lithographic reproduction. In top margin: 'STATIONERS' COMPANY'S ALMANAC FOR 1934'. In margin below almanack text: 'PUBLISHED BY THE WORSHIPFUL COMPANY OF STATIONERS, STATIONERS' HALL, E.C.4, AND TO BE OBTAINED FROM CHARLES LETTS & CO., SOUTHWARK BRIDGE BUILDINGS, LONDON S.E.1, OR ANY BOOKSELLER'.

Copies seen: CUL; LMA-GL

1892

KENSINGTON PALACE

Drawn by R. T. Pritchett.

Engraved by Herbert E. Sedcole.

192 × 370 mm

Steel engraving

In top margin: 'STATIONERS' COMPANY'S [arms] ALMANAC FOR 1892'. Pritchett's monogram in image at bottom right. In bottom margin, below almanack text: 'Printed by HARRISON AND SONS, Printers in Ordinary to Her Majesty, St. Martin's Lane, for the STATIONERS' COMPANY, Stationers' Hall, Ludgate Hill, London. Price Two Shillings'. An advertisement placed in the *British Almanac* for 1892 states that proof impressions of the engraving, on thick paper, could be purchased for 3s.

View of the palace taken from the east side of the Round Pond in Kensington Gardens. On the left is the tower and spire of St Mary Abbots, modelled on St Mary Redcliffe, Bristol. The State Apartments of the Palace had been opened to the public in 1889, and it was here that the London Museum would be housed. From 1880 until 1939 Kensington Palace was the home of Princess Louise, Queen Victoria's sixth child.

Copies seen: LMA-GL; SC

1893

THE TOWER BRIDGE.

Drawn by R. T. Pritchett.

Engraved by Herbert E. Sedcole.

196 × 370.5 mm

Steel engraving

In top margin: 'STATIONERS' COMPANY'S [arms] ALMANAC FOR 1893'. Pritchett's monogram within the image at bottom right. In bottom margin, below the almanack text: 'Printed by HARRISON

Headpiece for 1899 Almanack (see State 2 of **1855**, p. 54). For this version the steel plate has been revised and updated. The print now shows the Clock Tower of the Houses of Parliament as actually built, rather than as envisaged. It also shows Westminster Pier, opened 1870, and New Scotland Yard, erected 1888-90.

AND SONS, Printers in Ordinary to Her Majesty, St. Martin's Lane, for the STATIONERS' COMPANY, Stationers' Hall, Ludgate Hill, London. Price Two Shillings'. An advertisement placed in the *British Almanac* for 1893 stated that proof impressions of the engraving on thick paper could be had for 3*s*.

Tower Bridge, designed by Sir John Wolfe-Barry (1836–1918) and Sir Horace Jones (1819–87), was opened by the Prince of Wales on 30 June 1894. Pritchett's drawing for this headpiece was presumably made in 1892. It is shown as the artist predicted it would appear when complete and its bascules raised. Traffic on either side of the bridge form queues whilst a tall vessel passes through.

Copies seen: CUL; LMA-GL; SC

1895

ST. SAVIOUR'S, SOUTHWARK.

Drawn by H. W. Brewer.

Engraved by Herbert E. Sedcole.

222 × 368 mm

Steel engraving

In top margin: 'STATIONERS' COMPANY'S [arms] ALMANAC FOR 1895'. Within the image at bottom right: 'H.W. Brewer'. In bottom margin, below almanack text: 'Printed by HARRISON AND SONS, Printers in Ordinary to Her Majesty, St. Martin's Lane, for the STATIONERS' COMPANY, Stationers' Hall, Ludgate Hill, London. Price Two Shillings'.

St Saviour's (or St Mary Overie) was begun in
1220. Many of the earliest engraved views of
London were taken from its tower. Towards
the end of the nineteenth century it was
decided the church should become the
cathedral of a new diocese for south London.
In anticipation of this Sir Arthur Blomfield
(1829–99) designed a new nave, and the Prince
of Wales laid the foundation stone for it in
1890. St Saviour's was officially made the pro-
cathedral in 1897.

Copies seen: LMA-GL; SC

1900

THE NEW GOVERNMENT OFFICES

215 × 450

Steel engraving

In top margin: 'THE IMPERIAL. STATIONERS'
COMPANY'S [arms] ALMANAC FOR 1900. THE
IMPERIAL'. In bottom margin below the almanack
text: Printed and Published for the Stationer's
Company, London, by CHARLES LETTS & CO., 3,
Royal Exchange, E.C.

The building, designed by John McKean
Brydon (1840–1901) was erected 1898–1900.
This image of it was reproduced from one of
Brydon's published drawings, 1899. The
towers in Charles Street never materialized;

nor did the tower shown on the Home Office
building (designed by J. O. Scott) on the right;
and nor did the quadriga on the arch linking
the Local Government Board (on the left) with
the Home Office (on the right). The new
offices housed the Local Government Board,
the Board of Education, and (eventually) the
Board of Trade.

Copies seen: LMA-GL

APPENDIX

A LIST OF *LONDON ALMANACKS* WITH ENGRAVED LONDON HEADPIECES

In the 1670s the Stationers' Company began to regularly publish a small and convenient sheet displaying useful information. It was called the *Calendarium Londinense Verum* or *Raven's Almanack* and by the end of the century the *London Almanack*. An attractive feature of the publication was its engraved headpiece. Initially it consisted of an allegorical design, but in 1706, perhaps by way of an experiment, allegory gave way to a view of the Royal Exchange. In the following year the subject was Westminster Hall. By 1709 allegorical designs were back, and it was not until 1736 that London topographical views were this time seriously reintroduced and became a regular feature. The Stationers' Company continued to publish the *London Almanack*, year by year, virtually all with a London view, right until 1895. There are 152 of them in all. They constitute a valuable image bank.

1706
Royal Exchange of London. Almanack engraver: J. Nutting. (GL; SC)
In the top margin: 'Our Loyalty is the High-Road To a full Trade; at home & abroad'.

1707
Westminster-Hall. (GL*; YCBA)

1725
Stationers' Hall. (GL; P)

1736
[Prospect of the City of London from St Saviour's Southwark]. (GL)

1737
Cripple-Gate Lud-Gate New-Gate. (SC)

1738
Alders Gate and Moor Gate. (GL)

1739
Bishops-Gate Aldgate New-Gate. (BL*; SC)

1740
Guild-Hall [exterior]. (GL*; SC)

1741
Inside of Guild-Hall. (SC)

1742
Custom House. (SC)

1743
The Tower of London. (SC)

1744
Beth lem. (SC)

1745
Navy Office. Anon. (SC)

1746
Charter House. (GL; GL*; SC)

1747
Aske's Hospital. (GL*; SC)

1748
Christ's Hospital. (BodL; SofA; SC)

1749
St. Paul's School. (GL*; SofA; SC)

1750
The Mansion House. (BL*; GL*; SofA; SC)

1751
The Foundling Hospital. (GL*; SofA; SC)

1752
The Archbishop of Canterbury's Palace at Lambeth. (SofA; SC)

1753
Ironmongers' Hall. (BL*; LMA; GL; SofA; SC; SC*)

1754
A View of the Horse Guards. (BL*; SofA; SC)

1755
Buckingham House. (SofA; SC)

1756
Greenwich Hospital. (GL; SofA; SC)

1757
The British Museum or Late Montague House. (GL; SofA; SC*)

1758
The inside of the Church of St. Stephen Walbrook Sir Chrisr. Wren Kt Architect. Anon. (BL*; SofA; SC)

1759
The London Hospital. (BL*; ML*; SofA; SC)

1760
Marlborough House in St. James's Park. (SofA; SC)

1761
The Corn Market in Mark Lane. (SofA; SC)

1762
The Surgeons-Theatre in the Old-Bailey. (SofA; SC; SC*)

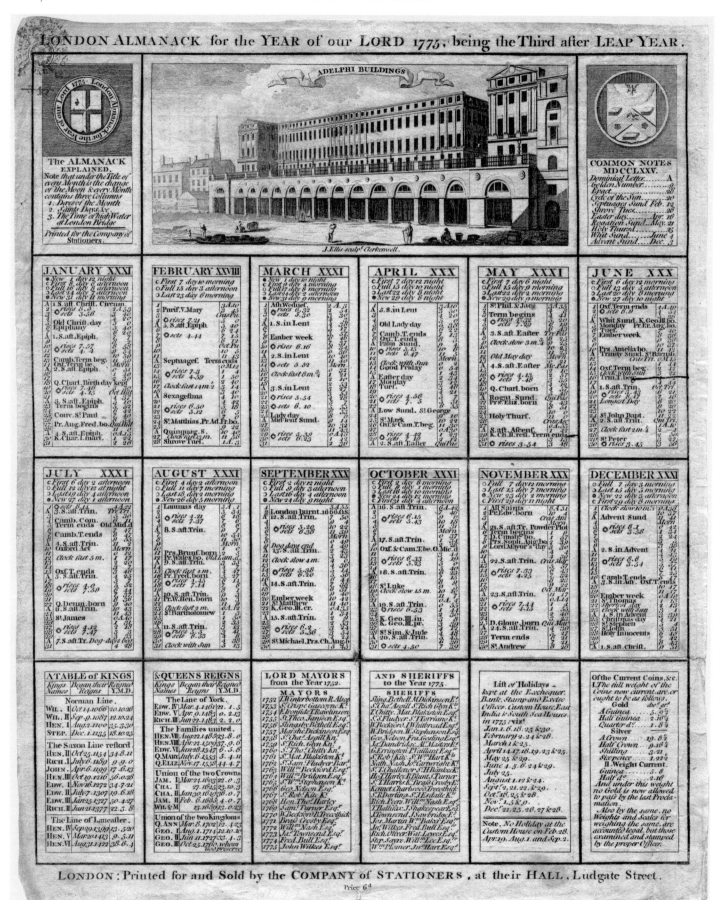

London Almanack sheet designed to be folded or dissected. Line engraving. 260 x 210 mm.

1763

London Bridge. (GL*; SofA; SC)

1764

Somerset House. (SofA; SC)

1765

Inside of the Royal Exchange. (BL*; SofA; SC)

1766

Black Fryars Bridge. (BL*; SofA; SC)

1767

The Bank. (GL*; ML*; SofA; SC)

1768

The East India House. (SofA; SC)

1769

Westminster Bridge. (BL*; SofA; SC; SC*)

1770

South Sea House. (SofA; SC)

1771

St Bartholomew's Hospital. (SofA; SC)

1772

The New Excise Office. (BL*; LMA-GL; SofA; SC; SC*)

1773

The City of London Lying-In Hospital. J. Ellis sculp. (LMA-GL; SofA)

1774

The New Sessions House. J. Ellis sculp. (BL*; GL; SofA; SC)

1775

Adelphi Buildings. J. Ellis sculp. (GL; SofA; SC; SC*)

1776

The Admiralty. J. Ellis sculp. Sold by George Hawkins. (BL*; BodL; SofA; SC)

1777

A View of Somerset House, from the River Thames. J. Ellis. Sold by George Hawkins. (BL*; SofA; SofA*; SC; SC*)

1778

A View of Westminster Hall, from New Palace Yard. J. Ellis sculp. Sold by George Hawkins. (BL*; GL*; SofA; SC)

1779

New Offices in the Strand formerly Somerset House. Carter del. Ellis sculp. Sold by George Hawkins. (BL*; BodL; GL*; SofA; SC).
Related pen-and-wash drawing in P.

1780

Back Front of the New Offices in the Strand lately Somerset House. Anon. Sold by George Hawkins. (BL*; BodL; GL*; SA; SC)

1781

Stationers' Hall. [John Carter del.]. Sold by John Wilkie. (BL*; BodL; ML*; SofA; SC; SC*)
The Stationers' Company have Carter's drawing. It is dated 14 June 1780. They also have a receipt from Wilkie for the payment to Carter of two guineas.

1782

Entrance into the Pantheon, Oxford Street taken from the Music Gallery. Anon. Sold by John Wilkie. (BL*; BodL; GL*; SC; SC*)

1783

Ordnance Office, Old Palace Yard. Carter del. Sold by John Wilkie. (BL*; BodL; GL*; SofA; SC)

1784

A View of Old Palace Yard, Westminster. Anon. Sold by John Wilkie. (BL*; Bodl; GL; SofA; SC)

1785

View of Somerset Place from the River Thames. J. Carter del. Sold by John Wilkie. (BL*; GL*; ML*; SofA; SC)

1786

View of the Bank of England, Threadneedle Street. Carter del. Sold by Robert Horsfield. (BL*; GL*; SofA; SC)

1787

Apothecaries Hall, Black Friars. Carter del. Sold by Robert Horsfield. (BL*; SofA; SC; SC*)

1788

South west View of St. Luke's Hospital for Lunaticks, in Old Street. Carter del. Ellis sc. Sold by Robert Horsfield. (BL*; GL*; SC; SC*)

1789

Carleton House [i.e., Carlton House], the Residence of His Royal Highness the Prince of Wales. Anon. Sold by Robert Horsfield. (LMA-GL; SC; SC*)

1790

York House the Residence of His Royal Highness the Duke of York. J. Carter del. Sold by Robert Horsfield. (BL: GL*)

1791

View of the Queen's Lodge and Castle at Windsor. Anon. Sold by Robert Horsfield. (BL*; SC)

1792

Guild-Hall, London. Anon. Sold by Robert Horsfield. (BL*; GL; GL*; ML*; SC)

1793

View of the New House of Correction for the County of Middlesex. J. Ellis sculp. Sold by Robert Horsfield. (BL*; GL*; SC; SC*)

1794

View of the Coal Exchange, Thames Street. Almanack engraver: B. Baker. Sold by Robert Horsfield. (BL*; GL*; SC)

1795

View of Drury Lane Theatre. Almanack engraver: B.

Baker. Sold by Robert Horsfield. (BL*; GL*; ML*; SC)

1796
View of the inside of the Hall at Carlton House. Almanack engraver: B. Baker. Sold by Robert Horsfield. (BL*; BM; ML*; SC; SC*)

1797
View of the Trinity House Tower Hill. Almanack engraver: B. Baker. Sold by Robert Horsfield. (BL*; GL; GL*; SC)

1798
View of Westminster Abbey from Lambeth. Almanack engraver: B. Baker. Sold by George Greenhill. (BL*; GL*; SC)

1799
View of St. Paul's and Black Friars Bridge. Almanack engraver: B. Baker. Sold by George Greenhill. (BL*; BodL; GL*; SC; SC*)

1800
View of the New Front of the East India House. Almanack engraver: B. Baker. Sold by George Greenhill. (BL*; LMA-GL; SC)

1801
View of Guildford Street from Queen Square. Almanack engraver: B. Baker. Sold by George Greenhill. (GL; SC; SC*)

1802
View of Brunswick Square. Almanack engraver: B. Baker. Sold by George Greenhill. (GL; GL*; SC)

1803
View of Stationers' Hall and the Adjacent Buildings. Almanack engraver: B. Baker. Sold by George Greenhill. (SC)

1804
View of the West India Docks from Blackwall Entrance. Almanack engraver: B. Baker. Sold by George Greenhill. (SC)

1805
View of the Royal Military Asylum Chelsea. Almanack engraver: B. Baker. Sold by George Greenhill. (SC)

1806
View of the London Docks. Almanack engraver: B. Baker. Sold by George Greenhill. (SC; SC*)

1807
North West View of Russell Square. Almanack engraver: B. Baker. Sold by George Greenhill. (BL*; GL*; SC)

1808
View of the House of Lords. Anon. Almanack engraver: B. Baker. Sold by George Greenhill. (BL*; GL*; SC; SC*)

1809
View of the Royal Military Academy, Woolwich, at Woolwich. Almanack engraver: B. Baker. Sold by George Greenhill. (SC; SC*)

1810
View of the Naval Asylum, at Greenwich. Almanack engraver: B. Baker. Sold by George Greenhill. (SC)

1811
View of Covent-Garden Theatre. Almanack engraver: B. Baker. Sold by George Greenhill. (SC)

1812
View of the New-Mint, Tower Hill. Almanack engraver: B. Baker. Sold by George Greenhill. (GL*)

1813
View of the Drury Lane Theatre. Almanack engraver: B. Baker. Sold by George Greenhill. (SC; SC*)

1814
View, of the Royal College of Surgeons in Lincolns Inn Fields. Almanack engraver: B. Baker. Sold by George Greenhill. (GL*; ML*; SC; Well)

1815
View of the Strand Bridge and the Thames. June 13th 1814 when the Allied Sovereigns visited Woolwich. Almanack engraver: B. Baker Sold by George Greenhill. (GL*; SC)

1816
View of the New Bethlem Hospital, St. Georges Fields. Almanack engraver: B. Baker. Sold by George Greenhill. (GL*; SC)

1817
View of Westminster Abbey, &c. with the Recent Improvements. Anon. Almanack engraver: B. Baker. Sold by George Greenhill. (BL*; GL*)

1818
View of the New Custom House, from the River. Almanack engraver: B. Baker. Sold by George Greenhill. (SC)

1819
Vauxhall Bridge with a View, of the Penitentiary at Millbank. Almanack engraver: B. Baker. Sold by George Greenhill. (GL; SC)

1820
View of the London Institution; Moorfields. Almanack engraver: B. Baker. Sold by George Greenhill. (LMA-GL; SC)

1821
View of the Southwark Bridge. Almanack engraver: B. Baker. Sold by George Greenhill. (BL*; SC)

1822
View of Furnivals Inn, Holborn. Almanack engraver: B. Baker. Sold by George Greenhill. (BodL; ML*; SC; SC*)

1823
View of the Quadrant in Regents Street. Almanack

engraver: B. Baker. Sold by George Greenhill. (SC; SC*)

1824
A View of St. Pancras New Church. Almanack engraver: B. Baker. Sold by George Greenhill. (BL*; SC)

1825
View of Saint Paul's School. Almanack engraver: B. Baker. Sold by George Greenhill. (BL*; SC)

1826
View of Richmond Terrace, Whitehall. Almanack engraver: B. Baker. Sold by George Greenhill. (SC)

1827
View of the Duke of York's House, in the Green Park. Almanack engraver: B. Baker. Sold by George Greenhill. (SC; SC*)

1828
The Grand Entrance of Hyde Park and the Lodge of the Kings Palace. Almanack engraver: B. Baker. Sold by George Greenhill. (SC)

1829
The New Hall, Christ's Hospital. H. Adlard sculp. Almanack engraver: B. Baker. Sold by George Greenhill. (SC)

1830
The Kings Palace, St James Park. T.M. Baynes del. H. Adlard sculp. Almanack engraver: B. Baker. Sold by George Greenhill. (ML*; SC)

1831
View of the New Bridge, in Hyde Park. H. Adlard sculp. Almanack engraver: B. Baker. Sold by George Greenhill. (GL*; SC)

1832
St. Katharine's Hospital and Chapel, Regent's Park. Almanack engraver: B. Baker. Sold by George Greenhill. (SC)

1833
New Hungerford Market. R. W. Billings del. H. Adlard sculp. Almanack engraver: B. Baker. Sold by George Greenhill. (SC)

1834
View of the New Grammar-School, Christ's Hospital. Almanack engraver: B. Baker. Sold by George Greenhill. (SC)

1835
View of New Goldsmith's Hall, Foster Lane. (GL*; SC)

1836
The New National Gallery. H. Adlard sculp. (SC)

1837
View of St. George's Hospital, Hyde Park Corner. (SC; SC*)

1838
The City of London School. (SC)

1839
The New School for the Indigent Blind, St. George's Fields. (SC)

1840
St. Saviour's Church, St. Thomas's Hospital, &c. in the Approach to London Bridge. (GL*; SC; SC*)

1841
The West or Garden Front of Buckingham Palace. (BL*; SC)

1842
Terminus of the Blackwall Railway [at Blackwall]. Sold by George Greenhill. (BL*; SC)

1843
Sun Fire Office, Threadneedle Street. J. Marchant del. H. Adlard sculp. Sold by George Greenhill. (BL*; GL; SC)

1844
The New Royal Exchange. J. Marchant del. H. Adlard. Sold by George Greenhill. (BodL; GL; SA)

1845
The Houses of Parliament. Sold by George Greenhill. (BL*; GL; SC)
Building not as built.

1846
Richmond Hill from Twickenham Meadows. J. Marchant del. H. Adlard sculp. Sold by George Greenhill. (BL*; GL*; SC)

1847
Infant Orphan Asylum Wanstead. H. Adlard sculp. Sold by George Greenhill. (BL*; GL; SC)

1848
The Orphan Working School, Haverstock Hill. H. Adlard sculp. Sold by George Greenhill. (GL; SC)

1850
Fishmongers and Poulterers Institution, Wood Green, Tottenham. J. Brown del. W.Webb archt. H. Adlard sculp. Sold by Joseph Greenhill. (GL; SC)

1851
Mansions of Earl Spencer and the Earl of Ellesmere [i.e., Spencer House and Bridgewater House] in the Green Park. H. Adlard sculp. Sold by Joseph Greenhill. (GL; SC)

1852
The Marble Arch, Cumberland Gate, Hyde Park. H. Adlard sculp. Sold by Joseph Greenhill. (GL; SC)

1855
Holland House, Kensington. H. Adlard sculp. Sold by Joseph Greenhill. (GL; ML*; SC)

1856
The Commercial Travellers' School – Pinner. P.

Phillips del. H. Adlard sculp. Sold by Joseph Greenhill. (GL; GL*; SC)

1857

The New Chelsea Bridge, leading to Battersea Park. H. Adlard sculp. Sold by Joseph Greenhill. (GL; SC)

1858

Ornamental Water and New Foot-Bridge in St. James's Park. P. Phillips del. H. Adlard sculp. Sold by Joseph Greenhill. (GL; SC)

1860

Chelsea Hospital from Battersea Park. H. Adlard sculp. Sold by Joseph Greenhill. (GL; SC)

1862

The Temperate House Royal Botanic Gardens, Kew. H. Adlard sculp. Sold by Joseph Greenhill. (GL; ML*; SC; SC*)

1863

Royal Humane Society's Receiving House, Hyde Park. H. Adlard sculp. Sold by Joseph Greenhill. (GL; ML*; SC)

1864

Victoria Park, Fountain Presented by Miss Burdett Coutts. H. Adlard sculp. Sold by Joseph Greenhill. (SC)

1866

The Albert Memorial — Hyde Park. P. Justyne del. H. Adlard sculp. Sold by Joseph Greenhill. (BL*; GL; SC; SC*)

1867

Royal Masonic Institution for Boys, Wood Green — Tottenham. P. Justyne del. H. Adlard sculp. Sold by Joseph Greenhill. (GL; ML*; SC)

1869

Alexandra Park Palace. P.W. Justyne del. H. Adlard sculp. Sold by Joseph Greenhill. (GL; SC)

1870

Metropolitan Meat Market. P. Justyne del. H. Adlard sculp. Sold by Joseph Greenhill. (GL; GL*; SC)

1871

New St. Thomas's Hospital. P. Justyne del. H. Adlard sculp. Sold by Joseph Greenhill. (GL; SC)

1872

Albert Hall and International Exhibition. P.W. Justyne del. H. Adlard sculp. Sold by Joseph Greenhill. (GL; SC)

1874

City Library and Museum [i.e., Guildhall Library & Museum]. P.W. Justyne del. H. Adlard sculp. Sold by Joseph Greenhill. (GL; SC)

1875

Dulwich College. Sold by Joseph Greenhill. (GL; SC)

1876

Alexandra Palace. Sold by Joseph Greenhill. (GL; ML*; SC)

1877

Kensington Palace. Sold by Joseph Greenhill. (GL; SC)

1879

Chelsea Embankment. Sold by Joseph Greenhill. (GL; SC)

1880

Cleopatra Needle (from the Thames). Sold by Joseph Greenhill's. (GL; SC)

1881

New Barracks, Knightsbridge. Sold by Joseph Greenhill. (GL; SC)

1882

Natural History Museum, Kensington. Sold by Joseph Greenhill. (GL; SC)

1883

City of London School. Anon. Sold by Joseph Greenhill. (GL; SC)

1884

Fishmongers' Hall. (GL; SC)

1885

City and Guilds of London Institute. (GL; SC)

1886

St. Paul's School, Hammersmith. Printed by Gilbert & Rivington Ltd. (GL; SC)

1887

Chelsea Hospital. Printed by Gilbert & Rivington Ltd. (BL*; GL; SC)

1888

People's Palace, Mile End. Printed by Gilbert & Rivington Ltd. (GL; SC)

1889

St. James' Palace. Printed by Gilbert & Rivington Ltd. (GL; SC)

1891

The Imperial Institute. Printed by Gilbert & Rivington Ltd. (GL; SC)

1892

The Church House. Printed by Gilbert & Rivington Ltd. (GL; SC)

1893

Victoria Embankment. Printed by Gilbert & Rivington. (GL; SC)

The *London Almanack* headpieces in 1894 and 1895 were half-tones. From 1896 the *London Almanack* was published, not by the Stationers' Company, but by Messrs Peacock, Mansfield & Britton of 18 Salisbury Square.

Examples of *London Almanacks* housed in covers and slip-cases and bound as minature books.

BIBLIOGRAPHY

Adams, Bernard, *London Illustrated, 1604–1851* (London: Library Association, 1983)

Barker, Felix, and Jackson, Peter, *London: 2000 Years of a City and its People* (London: Cassell & Co., 1974)

Blagden, Cyprian, *The Distribution of Almanacks in the Second Half of the Seventeenth Century*, Papers of the Bibliographical Society of Virginia, 11 (1958), pp. 107–16

Bosanquet, Eustace F., *English Printed Almanacks and Prognostications: A Bibliographic History to the Year 1600* (London: Bibliographical Society, 1917)

Capp, Bernard, *Astrology and the Popular Print: English Almanacks, 1500–1800* (London: Faber & Faber, 1979)

Bowden, R., 'The English Stock and the Stationers' Company', in R. Myers (ed.) *The Stationers' Company* ... (London: Worshipful Company of Stationers and Newspaper Makers, 2001), pp. 79–105

Catalogue of the Library of Miniature Books Collected by Percy Edwin Spielman (London: Arnold Press, 1961)

Chandler, John H., and Dagnall, H., *The Newspaper & Almanac Stamps of Great Britain & Ireland* (Saffron Waldon: Great Britain Philatelic Society, 1981)

Colvin, H. M., *A Biographical Dictionary of British Architects* (New Haven and London: Yale University Press, 1995)

Dagnall, H., *Creating a Good Impression: Three Hundred Years of the Stamp Office and Stamp Duties* (London: HMSO, 1994)

Galinou, Mireille, and Hayes, John, *London in Paint* (London: Museum of London, 1996)

'A Handlist of Almanacs in the Guildhall Library', *Guildhall Miscellany* (Aug. 1956)

Hyde, Ralph, 'William Monk's Calendar: Time to Say Goodbye', *Print Quarterly* (June 2000), pp. 132–47

Kettle, Bernard, *Stationers' Company's Almanacs* (London: Printed by students attending St Bride Foundation Printing School, 1922)

'London Almanacs', *Miniature Books News* (Sept. 1990)

'London Almanac Sizes', *Miniature Book News* (Dec. 1965)

Myers, Robin, 'The Stationers' Company & the Almanack Trade', in *The Cambridge History of the Book in Britain* Vol 5 (Cambridge University Press, 2009)

Osborne, Michael, *The State Barges of the Stationers' Company* (London: Company of Stationers and Newspaper Makers, 1972)

Perrett, Bryan, *The Battle Book* (London: Arms & Armour Press, 1992)

Petter, Helen Mary, *The Oxford Almanacks* (Oxford: Clarendon Press, 1974)

Weinreb, Ben, et al., *The London Encyclopaedia* (London: Macmillan, 2008)

ILLUSTRATION CREDITS

NAME INDEX

PLACE INDEX